RE ADING AND INTERPRETING THE BIBLE SERIES

THE PAULINE EPISTLES

DAVID A. ACKERMAN

f

THE FOUNDRY
PUBLISHING

The Foundry Publishing®
PO Box 419527
Kansas City, MO 64141
thefoundrypublishing.com

ISBN 978-0-8341-4051-6

Cover design: J.R. Caines
Interior design: Jody Langley

Unless otherwise indicated, all Scripture quotations are from the Holy Bible, New International Version® (NIV®). Copyright © 1973, 1978, 1984, 2011 by Biblica, Inc.™ Used by permission of Zondervan. All rights reserved worldwide. www.zondervan.com. The "NIV" and "New International Version" are trademarks registered in the United States Patent and Trademark Office by Biblica, Inc.™

The following version of Scripture is in the public domain:
The King James Version (KJV)

The following copyrighted versions of Scripture are used by permission:
The Holy Bible, Berean Study Bible, BSB. Copyright © 2016, 2020 by Bible Hub. All Rights Reserved Worldwide.

The ESV® Bible (The Holy Bible, English Standard Version®), copyright © 2001 by Crossway, a publishing ministry of Good News Publishers. All rights reserved.

The New American Standard Bible® (NASB®), copyright © 1960, 1971, 1977, 1995, 2020 by The Lockman Foundation. All rights reserved. www.lockman.org.

The New King James Version® (NKJV). Copyright © 1982 by Thomas Nelson. All rights reserved.

The Holy Bible, New Living Translation (NLT), copyright © 1996, 2004, 2015 by Tyndale House Foundation. Used by permission of Tyndale House Publishers, Carol Stream, Illinois 60188. All rights reserved.

The New Revised Standard Version Bible (NRSV), copyright © 1989 National Council of the Churches of Christ in the United States of America. All rights reserved worldwide.

Scripture quotations marked TNT are from *The Translator's New Testament*. Edited by William McHardy. London: British and Foreign Bible Society, 1973.

Library of Congress Cataloging-in-Publication Data

Names: Ackerman, David A., 1966- author.
Title: The Pauline Epistles / David A. Ackerman.
Description: Kansas City, MO : The Foundry Publishing, [2022] | Series: Reading and interpreting the Bible series | Includes bibliographical references. | Summary: "Author David Ackerman shows that a proper approach to interpreting Paul's letters will help bridge the gap between Paul's world and ours, and separate the timeless from the time bound. Readers are introduced to Paul's social world, life, and mission, and clear explanations and illustrations using challenging texts equip the reader with the tools to better understand Paul's writings"-- Provided by publisher.
Identifiers: LCCN 2021049308 (print) | LCCN 2021049309 (ebook) | ISBN 9780834140516 (paperback) | ISBN 9780834140523 (ebook)
Subjects: LCSH: Bible. Epistles of Paul--Criticism, interpretation, etc.
Classification: LCC BS2650.52 .A25 2022 (print) | LCC BS2650.52 (ebook) | DDC 227/.06--dc23/eng/20220106
LC record available at https://lccn.loc.gov/2021049308
LC ebook record available at https://lccn.loc.gov/2021049309

The internet addresses, email addresses, and phone numbers in this book are accurate at the time of publication. They are provided as a resource. The Foundry Publishing® does not endorse them or vouch for their content or permanence.

In memory of my parents, Daniel and Dorothy Ackerman,
who instilled in me a love for Scripture
through their own quiet study and example

Contents

Abbreviations

General

d.	died
Eng.	English
Ger.	German
Gk.	Greek
Lat.	Latin
lit.	literally
r.	reigned

Modern Translations

AT	author's translation
BSB	Berean Study Bible
ESV	English Standard Version
KJV	King James Version
NASB	New American Standard Bible
NIV	New International Version
NKJV	New King James Version
NLT	New Living Translation
NRSV	New Revised Standard Version
TNT	The Translator's New Testament

Apocrypha

Wis.	Wisdom of Solomon

Old Testament Pseudepigrapha

4 Ezra	*4 Ezra*

Dead Sea Scrolls

1QH	*Thanksgiving Hymns*
1QM	*War Scroll*
1QS	*Rule of the Community*

Introduction

Becoming Interpreters of Paul

Paul's letters have challenged readers from the earliest days of the church. Although written long ago, these letters still speak to us, but we must approach them with care and openness. As with the original readers, we may find our worldviews challenged, our behaviors critiqued, and, ultimately, our lives changed to be more as God intends. This was undoubtedly Paul's intention and goal for the early churches. He believed the gospel calls people from the old life controlled by sin and self to a new life of faith in Jesus Christ. When a person enters into a relationship with Jesus Christ and experiences the transforming leadership of the Holy Spirit in the obedience of faith, all of that person's life is impacted.

Paul's letters are not easy to understand. Second Peter 3:15-16 expresses what many people have felt throughout the ages: "Bear in mind that our Lord's patience means salvation, just as our dear brother Paul also wrote you with the wisdom that God gave him. He writes the same way in all his letters, speaking in them of these matters. His letters contain some things that are hard to understand, which ignorant and unstable people distort, as they do the other Scriptures, to their own destruction." Verse 16 gives us several clues about how the early church received Paul's letters.

First, although Paul wrote his letters over many years and in different situations, they are united in their primary message of God's salvation through Jesus Christ. Although the authenticity of certain letters has been questioned (Ephesians, Colossians, 2 Thessalonians, 1 and 2 Timothy, and Titus), a case can be made that there is a strong unity of thought behind all thirteen canonical letters attributed to Paul.

Second, Paul's letters are often "hard to understand." His use of rhetoric often leads people to think that he is making a circular argument or contradicting himself. Reading only a small unit or isolated verse can bring confusion, especially in long and complex letters, such as Romans. It takes effort to read an entire letter and consider the overall argument and context in order to understand the smaller parts.

Third, those who lack understanding may too easily misinterpret the letters and distort their meaning. Since such misinterpretation happened so soon after the letters were written in the early years of the church, among people who shared the same culture and language, it should not surprise us that this still happens in our own day. To read and understand Paul's letters clearly and accurately takes significant effort and careful methodology. Peter minces no words when he shows what is at stake in interpreting Paul's letters accurately: *avoiding destruction!* This can be put more positively: we must interpret these ancient letters faithfully and accurately because we believe that God still speaks through them to us, showing the way to eternal salvation. They deserve our best thinking, our best study skills, and our openness to hear the Holy Spirit bring fresh life in them for us today.

Contemporary Wesleyan Approaches

In the last one hundred years, many new methods of studying the Bible have emerged. Many of these have proven helpful for interpreting Paul's letters. Wesleyan scholars have generally embraced the best that new scholarship offers but also weigh this with what has been written in the past. In the so-called Wesleyan quadrilateral,[1] the three secondary authorities bring vital tools to the superior authority, *Scripture*: *reason* as the careful use of interpretive methods, *tradition* as the voice of the church throughout the ages, and *experience* as the dynamic mission of the Holy Spirit in persons and groups. Leaving any one of these components out of this method of theological reflection will lead to imbalance.

An important step when reading Paul's letters is to ask good questions. Some questions may be interesting to ask but have no clear answer in what Paul actually wrote. People are quite creative in speculating about what he may have meant. A more valid approach is to determine what can be known with certainty and then only cautiously consider possible meanings. There is plenty in Paul's letters that is clear. With careful and thorough consideration, even some of the unclear passages can begin to take on more meaning.

The goal of this book is to give readers tools to use in their own study of the Pauline Epistles. Various approaches are used to investigate different types of literary genres within the letters. These chapters are meant to be illustrative and not definitive. I have chosen several of the more challenging texts in order to demonstrate viable ways to understand and draw meaning for our lives today. It is naïve to think that anyone can simply pick up Paul's letters and understand everything he wrote. The gulf of time, culture, and language is too great for us to presume we can penetrate the depths of his thought without careful study.

As with all Scripture study, there are basic hermeneutical assumptions and methods that guide us in this book. One important assumption is that we share in the same community as that of Paul: the one people

---

1. The Wesleyan quadrilateral refers to a summation of John Wesley's "view of religious authority," with Scripture being the preeminent authority over reason, tradition, and experience, which are secondary. The description was coined by Wesleyan scholar Albert Outler in the 1960s. See Don Thorsen, "Quadrilateral, Wesleyan," in *Global Wesleyan Dictionary of Theology*, ed. Al Truesdale (Kansas City: Beacon Hill Press of Kansas City, 2013), 443-44.

of God who have found new life in our relationship with Jesus Christ. When Paul was writing to the early church, he was also writing to us. We share in Paul's theological vision.[2] This makes these letters alive. God spoke through Paul long ago and now speaks to us through the accepted canon of Scripture.

Another assumption is that we can use many tools of exegesis to interpret these letters. There are basic tools or practices that should be considered with any part of the Bible, including personally translating from the original language when possible (or comparing modern translations), examining word studies and the usage of words within their contexts, analyzing the flow of thought and the literary context, researching the background and historical situation, analyzing the grammar and how the words relate to each other, identifying the major themes and theological messages, and assessing how all this applies to our lives today as God's word. Scholars have drawn upon methods used in other settings to aid in their study of Paul's letters, including literary, rhetorical, and social-scientific methods. As Wesleyans, we embrace these methods but also recognize that they should support and lead to the message and not become ends in themselves.

The Importance of Paul for Christian Living Today

Many key Christian doctrines are explained and have their basis in Paul's letters. Yet Paul did not write as a theologian but as a combination pastor, church planter, and missionary. His approach to early church development should challenge us as readers to realize that our study of his letters should not result in abstract theological tomes but in engaged mission to our own communities. If we restrict our study to the abstract process of a pastor's office, library carrel, or professor's study, we will have

---

2. Joel B. Green, *Seized by Truth: Reading the Bible as Scripture* (Nashville: Abingdon Press, 2007), 18, 51.

missed the power of these letters. There is a place for theologizing, for helping the church go deep in its understanding, but to be true to Paul's spirit, this theology must lead to changed behavior (ethics), the evangelization of unbelievers, and the spiritual growth of believers. Paul was keenly interested in mentoring and training leaders wherever he went. An honest approach to his letters will challenge our worldviews and move us out of our comfort zones.

We will begin our study by considering Paul's background, methods, and key approach to his ministry. With this foundation, we will be better equipped to explore individual passages in order to hear once again a call to the holy and loving church of Jesus Christ.

1

Paul's Mission to the World
BACKGROUND AND SETTING

Paul, the Missionary Pastor

The threads of Paul's life form the background of the tapestry of his later ministry. Everyone, including Paul, is influenced by his or her background, family upbringing, cultural context, education, language, and choices in life. Although little is known about Paul's background, his letters and the book of Acts give us many clues that help us read his letters with more understanding.

In the interpretation process, a crucial step is to study the background of the author, audience, and general worldview behind the text. Every text has a certain timelessness to it, no matter how hidden behind the time-bound application this might be. We might label this timeless feature the *intended message* of the author. What effect does the author wish his or her writing to have upon the reader? In the world of literature, the desired effect might be to elicit entertainment or to bring about a deep spiritual encounter. However, the desired effect is often difficult to discover because the world of the reader is different from the world of the author. The closer the reader can get to the world of the text, the more meaningful the text will be to the reader and thus the greater the impact of the author's ideas upon the reader.

This is particularly true for the Bible and Paul's letters. Investigating Paul's background helps us to avoid imposing our own ideas, cultures, and worldviews on his letters. What we assume to be timeless may turn out to be written specifically to a time-bound situation. The more we know of the world of Paul and how he wrote his letters, the better we can discern the messages God intends for all cultures and times. Our ultimate goal is to hear God's message to us in such a way that we can respond with faith and obedience.

Called to the Gentile World

Before Paul was known as an apostle, he went by the name of Saul, also the name of the first king of Israel. Little is known about the early years of Saul's life except the few autobiographical references in his letters and the scarce hints in the book of Acts. Many scholars view the information in Acts as somewhat suspicious because it is secondhand information from Luke and not directly from Paul. The issue of the historical accuracy of Acts is complex. Luke was a careful writer (Luke 1:3) and accompanied Paul on several of his travels. In some passages of Acts, Luke uses "we" as the subject of the sentences (Acts 16:10-17; 20:5-15; 21:1-18; 27:1-37; 28:1-16). The assumption is that Luke was with Paul during those times, and so the information is firsthand. In other places, Luke would have investigated and learned about the events, either directly from Paul or someone close to the events. This all leads to the conclusion that Acts can still be a reliable source for reconstructing Paul's background.

Paul's letters contain several autobiographical sections where he uses his background to compare himself to false teachers who were either discrediting him or his message. In Philippians 3:5-6, he writes that he was "circumcised on the eighth day, of the people of Israel, of the tribe of Benjamin, a Hebrew of Hebrews; in regard to the law, a Pharisee; as for zeal, persecuting the church; as for righteousness based on the law, faultless." He had an outstanding pedigree for a first-century Jew. In Galatians

1:13-14, he writes, "For you have heard of my previous way of life in Judaism, how intensely I persecuted the church of God and tried to destroy it. I was advancing in Judaism beyond many of my own age among my people and was extremely zealous for the traditions of my fathers." Here, he connects his past life as a persecutor to his zeal for Jewish traditions. As an up-and-coming Pharisee, he put much effort into keeping the law as he understood it. This zeal led him to persecute the early followers of Jesus (Acts 7:54–8:1; 9:1-4; 1 Cor. 15:9; Gal. 1:13; Phil. 3:6; 1 Tim. 1:12-13). He believed these followers, known as the "Way" (Acts 9:2), were following a false messiah. He believed he was acting in the best way, although later he realized it was out of "ignorance and unbelief" (1 Tim. 1:13).

The book of Acts confirms much of Paul's background and fills in a few more details. We learn that he was from the city of Tarsus in Cilicia (Acts 9:11; 21:39; 22:3) and a Roman citizen, a significant privilege in that time that offered some protections (16:37-38; 22:25-29; 23:27). At some point, he was educated in Jerusalem under the famous rabbi Gamaliel (22:3). He knew Greek, the international language of the time, and Aramaic, the spoken language of Palestinian Jews (21:40; 22:2), and he could read the Hebrew Bible. He was a "young man" (7:58) when he persecuted the church, so he could have been born anytime between 5 BC and AD 10. He retained much of his Jewish upbringing, education, and worldview, although the next chapter of his life significantly altered this in a life-changing way.

The life of the young Saul was forever changed on a road trip to Damascus, where he intended to arrest the believers dwelling there. He was so adamant about erasing the heresy of the followers of Jesus that he asked for letters from the high priest in Jerusalem and then set out with murder in his eyes. This significant event is recounted three times in Acts: 9:1-19; 22:17-21; 26:12-18. On the way, he had a vision of the risen Jesus Christ, who told Saul that he was now called to go to the Gentile world with the message of good news about Christ. Saul's response was one of immediate obedience. The vision blinded him and sent him into deep prayer and contemplation of who this Jesus really was. This encounter with the true Messiah left a deep mark on his mind and heart and forever changed his outlook on life. His zeal for persecution was replaced by a passion to reach the lost. He believed his change from being the worst of sinners for his blasphemy, persecution of the church, and violence (1 Tim. 1:13) to being an apostle willing to suffer for the sake of Christ served as "an example for those who would believe in [Christ] and receive eternal life" (v. 16). This transforming encounter with Christ continued throughout Saul's life and ministry and was made vividly real and experiential through the power and presence of the indwelling Holy Spirit. Although this encounter with Christ changed everything about Saul, he could never fully escape his Jewish heritage. Rather, he saw this heritage as being fulfilled in Christ.

Missionary Journeys

The following years of Paul's life are somewhat obscure. It is difficult and even controversial to piece together a clear picture of the time line of his life based on his letters and the book of Acts. Acts provides a linear narrative of Paul's life after Damascus, with the purpose of informing Theophilus about the growth of the early church (Acts 1:1-2; Luke 1:1-4). Paul's letters give more of a synchronic or periodic look at key moments in order to call the early churches to action and orthodoxy. After some time in Damascus and possibly three more years in Arabia (Gal. 1:16-17; Acts 9:19-25), Paul may have made a brief fifteen-day return trip to Jerusalem to meet the followers residing there (Gal. 1:18-20; Acts 9:26-29). Then for fourteen years, he preached in Syria and his home area of Cilicia (Gal. 1:21–2:1; Acts 9:30). This may also be when he took his first missionary trip with Barnabas, described in Acts 13:4–15:35.

Paul returned to Jerusalem again to consult with the leaders there about the mission to the Gentiles (Gal. 2:1-10). It is possible but not undisputed that this was related to the Jerusalem Council of Acts 15. Paul then went on a second missionary journey with Silas, described in Acts 15:36–18:22. His final missionary journey took him to Jerusalem to deliver the offering he had taken up for the believers in that city (18:23–21:17). While there, he was arrested in the temple, imprisoned, and then sent to Caesarea, where he spent two years in the custody of the Romans. He was finally sent to Rome for a formal trial before the emperor (27:1–28:16). Acts ends with him under house arrest in Rome awaiting this trial. Nothing is known after this in the canonical record, but

> **Paul was a changed person who was driven by his call to preach the gospel in the Gentile world. This mission was compelled by "the love of Christ."**

church tradition states that Paul was finally tried before Nero and beheaded sometime in the mid-AD 60s. This chronology can be expanded significantly as attempts are made to fit in the various letters with Paul's journeys and imprisonments.

One thing becomes clear after reading Acts and then Paul's letters: Paul was a changed person who was driven by his call to preach the gospel in the Gentile world. This mission was compelled by "the love of Christ" (2 Cor. 5:14, NKJV) and Paul's deep and profound relationship with the risen Jesus Christ. His early zeal continued but was transformed and empowered through the Holy Spirit. His Jewish heritage was put through a new worldview of eternal hope and life made possible through Christ's death and resurrection.

When Paul went to a new place to preach the gospel, he primarily targeted the urban centers of the Roman Empire. These cities were full of polytheism and religious pluralism. They were multilingual, a mixture of many cultures, and economically stratified, with a few who were wealthy and many who were poor and slaves. He and his companions followed the leading of the Holy Spirit, who directed them on their mission to different cities (Acts 13:4; 16:6; 20:23). His usual strategy was to go to the Jewish synagogue or local gathering place for Jews. There he would proclaim Jesus to be the Messiah and used Scripture to reason with the people. In the synagogues, he also met "Godfearers," who believed in the God of Israel but were not ethnically related or circumcised (13:16, 26). Paul was welcomed in many places, and many people believed his message. But he also encountered significant opposition, especially from the Jews. During his time in Corinth, he finally reached the point of frustration and said, "Your blood be on your own heads! I am innocent of it. From now on I will go to the Gentiles" (18:6). He never gave up his hope that the Jews would come to faith in Jesus as the Messiah (Rom. 11).

Paul almost always had partners in ministry with him. They served in many roles to assist in the spread of the gospel. They helped him in the actual preaching and teaching in various locations. He left behind some at certain locations to continue to develop the local churches after he departed. At times, he sent an emissary to check on a church, carry a letter, or deal with a problem. These emissaries were his representatives and came with his authority as an apostle, and so he expected the churches to listen and receive the words of these people. When Paul was in prison, he especially relied on the assistance of those close to him. Several of his letters were coauthored by those who were present with him, including Silas and Timothy. The ideas in Paul's letters were not completely his own but shared among other early Christians. The extent of the involvement of these coauthors in Paul's letters is impossible to determine, but it is generally agreed that Paul was the primary author of the contents.

Up to ninety-five different coworkers are mentioned in Paul's letters and the book of Acts. Little is known about many of these except their names. A significant number, however, spent a considerable amount of time traveling with him, ministering with him in a city or church, or being sent by him on a commissioned journey. A smaller group might be considered ministry associates who worked specifically as part of the mission team. Barnabas and Mark accompanied him on his first missionary journey (Acts 13:1-3, 5). Titus joined them for a time (Gal. 2:1, 3). On the second missionary journey, Silas was Paul's primary partner after there was a disagreement between Paul and Barnabas about taking Mark on this second journey (Acts 15:36-40). As Paul went through Greece, the young Timothy and Luke joined him (16:1-3, 10). Other key partners are mentioned throughout Paul's letters, many of whom remained in close partnership with him until the end of his life (2 Tim. 4:10-12).

Hardships and Imprisonments

The first time Saul of Tarsus is mentioned in Acts, he is involved in the stoning of Stephen (7:58). At the next mention, he is bent on destroying the church and throwing believers into prison (8:3; 22:4, 19; 26:10). His zeal for ridding the land of Jesus's followers drove him next to get letters of authority to arrest more Christians in Damascus. Ironically, from the earliest days of his life as a believer, his own life was one of suffering. When the risen Jesus called Saul on the road to Damascus, this calling was not simply to preach the gospel but to suffer for Jesus's name (9:16). Soon after Saul's vision, he began to preach the gospel in Damascus. It took only a few days for opposition to rise against him to the point of him having to flee the city by being "lowered . . . in a basket through an opening in the wall" (v. 25).

Much of Paul's letters were written with the backdrop of suffering. It is difficult to understand his letters without appreciating his location as one who suffered for his faith. He experienced opposition throughout his ministry, especially from the Jews. Acts is full of references to his suffering, and every letter mentions some aspect of it. He gives an extensive catalog of suffering in 2 Corinthians 6:4-5; 11:23-29. According to the early Christian document *1 Clement*, written around the end of the first century, Paul was "seven times in chains."[1] Paul wrote some of his letters from prison, with tradition naming these the Prison Epistles: Ephesians, Philippians, Colossians, and Philemon. In addition, it is possible that Paul wrote 2 Timothy during his last imprisonment in Rome. He faced many hardships, such as hunger, poverty, beatings, rejection, and ridicule (1 Cor. 4:8-13; 2 Tim. 3:10-11).

Roman prisons were notorious for cruelty and inflicting pain upon those who were put in them. Paul's imprisonments were sometimes accompanied by beatings (Acts 16:23). His Roman citizenship often helped him escape the worse beatings or even death. He called upon his citizenship in his appeal to be tried before Caesar (22:25-29; 23:27). Whenever Paul refers to himself as a prisoner, it is always as a "prisoner of Christ Jesus" or a variation of this (Philem. vv. 1, 9; Eph. 3:1; 4:1; 2 Tim. 1:8). Even in his imprisonment, Paul recognized Jesus Christ as Lord and Sovereign and able to get him either released or to sustain him during his suffering. No matter what happened to him, Paul wrote with confidence: "For to me, to live is Christ and to die is gain" (Phil. 1:21). Through his hardship, Paul learned about God's grace, the power of prayer, and the importance of Christian community. He wrote to the Corinthians, "But he said to me, 'My grace is sufficient for you, for my power is made perfect in weakness.' Therefore I will boast all the more gladly about my weaknesses, so that Christ's power may rest on me. That is why, for Christ's sake, I delight in weaknesses, in insults, in hardships, in persecutions, in difficulties. For

---

1. *The Letter of the Romans to the Corinthians (1 Clement)* 5:6, in *The Apostolic Fathers*, trans. J. B. Lightfoot and J. R. Harmer, ed. Michael W. Holmes, 2nd ed. (Grand Rapids: Baker Book House, 1989), 31.

when I am weak, then I am strong" (2 Cor. 12:9-10). He saw his imprisonments as an opportunity to bear witness to the grace of Jesus Christ to the guards who may have been chained to him or watched over him (Acts 16:27-31; Phil. 1:12-13).

Paul believed that God allowed him to suffer so that he would come to know God's power more personally and vividly. It was through his weakness that he saw the power of the Holy Spirit at work (1 Cor. 2:1-5). Through his imprisonments, the gospel went out in ways it might not have otherwise (2 Cor. 2:14). Through his struggles, the power of Christ was more evident (4:11). Paul had the firm belief that this life is not our final destiny and that our goal is to be "at home with the Lord." Meanwhile, we must press forward in discipline and fervency, relying on the grace of Christ (5:6-9). Paul believed that the same power at work in Christ's resurrection was working in his life and would sustain him through any trial he faced. Paul recognized that his sufferings were not unique and that being a believer would bring suffering (Rom. 8:17). It is through suffering that we come to experience death to the old self and new life in Christ. Suffering offers opportunity for faith to grow, leading to character development and the strengthening of our faith (5:3-5). Paul developed a rich theology of suffering through the hardships he faced. He never turned his back from this, and he learned to lean on the grace of God and the generosity of other believers to sustain him until the end of his life.

Paul the Letter Writer

Staying in Contact

Once Paul had established a church and left for another mission opportunity, he kept in contact with the church by sending emissaries and writing letters. On some occasions, he was able to return for another visit to check on the situation in person. This continued contact had several purposes, including spiritual nurture, correction of false teaching, moral exhortation, clarification of his message in the face of misunderstandings, preparation for travel, and intercession for others, including taking up a major offering for those in Jerusalem suffering from a famine. Although a letter was not as effective as a personal visit, it still held a position of authority for him.[2] His letters served as substitutes for his personal presence and carried the same authority as if he were there in person. He carried on a dialogue with the churches by corresponding with letters that challenged the churches to grow in his teachings and lifestyle.

We look to Paul's letters today for their theological and ethical teaching, and so did the early church. The churches saw power and relevancy in these letters and so preserved them, made copies of them, and sent these copies to other churches. By the end of the first century, most of Paul's letters were circulating together as a collected group. The letters hint at the extent of Paul's extensive communication network, with mention of a significant range of places across the Roman Empire. He did not write abstract, theoretical, or theological treatises but addressed actual problems faced in the early churches. He wrote as a pastor to his churches, with deep concern for their spiritual welfare. His letters unified the churches around a common theology that decades and centuries later was determined as genuine orthodoxy. Because Paul's letters were occasional, written at specific points in time for specific situations, we do not get his complete thought (diachronic—the development of ideas over time) but only glimpses of his thinking for these situations (synchronic—the moments in a larger story). This makes it difficult to synthesize his theology into a logical system.

---

2. Robert Walter Funk, "The Apostolic *Parousia*: Form and Significance," in *Christian History and Interpretation: Studies Presented to John Knox*, ed. W. R. Farmer, C. F. D. Moule, and R. R. Niebuhr (Cambridge, UK: Cambridge University Press, 1967), 249.

The Parts of a Letter

The style of Paul's letters is similar to other ancient letters. Letter writing was a form of written communication that took the place of oral communication. Certain rules or "conventions" were developed by ancient rhetoricians to guide this communication. Paul adapted the conventions of his time to serve his own purposes in writing his letters. Knowing the basic structures and styles of speech and writing can be useful for interpreting Paul's letters.

There were two major types of ancient letters: official, sent to heads of state about affairs of state, and informal-personal, which is the type Paul followed. Paul's letters were more than personal letters; they were intended to influence the growth of the early church. He wrote with the authority of an apostle, and so this influenced how he constructed his letters. Ancient letters generally had three major parts that could be divided into smaller sections: opening, body, and conclusion. The following is a brief description of each part.

A letter opened with the salutation. It began by naming the sender (Paul) and sometimes a coauthor (Timothy, Sosthenes, etc.). Paul often includes a reference to his authority as an apostle or his relationship with Jesus Christ. The recipient is named next, which for Paul included both churches and individuals. This is followed by a greeting. Paul's typical greeting is "grace and peace," which is a combination of the Greek greeting (*chairein*, meaning "greetings" or "rejoice") and the Jewish greeting (*shalom*, "peace"). Paul's greeting is significant because he takes these typical greetings and fills them with theological meaning and shows that the sources of grace and peace are God the Father and the Lord Jesus Christ.

After the salutation comes the thanksgiving. Paul's thanksgivings may contain a mention of prayer to God, praise for something God has done for the individual or church, a statement of relationship, and often a hint of the contents of the letter. Paul often gives thanks for the topics or problems he addresses later in the letter. Interestingly, the thanksgiving is missing in Galatians, 2 Corinthians, 1 Timothy, and Titus—four letters where Paul is particularly dealing with heretical teachers.

The bodies of Paul's letters differ according to the topics and situations about which he wrote. The body takes up the bulk of the letter; a long letter may have multiple major units within the body. Paul often structured his letters carefully to highlight certain key thoughts he wanted to make explicitly clear. The bodies of his letters contain many elements of rhetoric described below.

The closing of the letter is often signaled by a blessing, greetings, and a final exhortation. Paul often mentions his travel plans and gives a prayer, wish, or benediction for the readers. Some letters include a personal reference from him as a form of signature to authenticate the letter.

Paul's Letters as Persuasion

Ancient letters were often seen as written speeches and show many characteristics similar to rhetorical communication. Demetrius of Phaleron (b. ca. 350 BC) wrote that "a letter ought to be written in the same manner as a dialogue, a letter being regarded . . . as one of the two sides of a dialogue. . . . The letter should be a little more studied than the dialogue, since the latter reproduces an extemporary utterance, while the former is committed to writing and is . . . sent as gift."[3] When Paul wrote his letters, rhetoric was one of the standard subjects of Greco-Roman education and provided the rules for public discourse. A quick reading of Paul's letters shows he had some level of training in rhetoric and had some familiarity with Greek and Latin works. His hometown of Tarsus had a famous rhetorical school, although there is no indication that he attended it. Not everyone

---

3. Demetrius, *Demetrius on Style: The Greek Text of Demetrius* De Elocutione, trans. W. Rhys Roberts, paras. 223-24 (Cambridge, UK: University Press, 1902), 173, https://www.google.com/books/edition/Demetrius_On_Style /gjEMAQAAIAAJ?hl=en&gbpv=1&dq.

was formally trained in the finer points of rhetorical theory, but most were exposed to rhetoric in the public arena in the Hellenistic culture. Burton Mack writes, "To be engulfed in the culture of Hellenism meant to have ears trained for the rhetoric of speech. Rhetoric provided the rules for making critical judgments in the course of all forms of social intercourse."[4]

Rhetorical criticism is a useful tool for interpreting Paul's letters because it helps us analyze how he wrote in order to communicate his message. Aristotle (fourth century BC) defined rhetoric as "the art of persuasion."[5] Rhetoric describes the way a speaker attempts to convince an audience of some purpose or to convince them to participate in the viewpoint or worldview of the speaker.[6] The "rhetorical situation" consists of the persons, circumstances, and relations that necessitate a verbal response. Discovering this helps determine the intended message of the speaker.

Aristotle identified five major elements of rhetoric.[7] The first element, *invention*, determines the best way to communicate by deciding how arguments are developed and what issues are to be argued in a discourse based on internal or external proofs. External proofs come from outside the speaker (e.g., quotations). Aristotle gave three modes of internal or artistic proof: *ethos, pathos,* and *logos. Ethos* centers on the moral character or credibility of the speaker, the trust in the speaker the audience has or develops. *Pathos* is the emotional response of the audience. *Logos* is the logical argument found in the discourse.

Three types of rhetoric are used with invention. *Judicial* rhetoric seeks to accuse, defend, or persuade about events that happened in the past. It involves the question of truth or justice and often was used in a courtroom. *Deliberative* rhetoric appeals to the audience to make the right

---

4. Burton L. Mack, *Rhetoric and the New Testament* (Minneapolis: Fortress Press, 1990), 31.

5. See Aristotle, *Aristotle's Treatise on Rhetoric*, bk. 1, ch. 2, trans. Theodore Buckley (London: Henry G. Bohn, 1850), 11-24, https://archive.org/details/aristotlestreat00aris/page/10/mode/2up.

6. Chaïm Perelman and L. Olbrechts-Tyteca, *The New Rhetoric: A Treatise on Argumentation* (Notre Dame, IN: University of Notre Dame, 1969).

7. Aristotle, *Rhetoric*, bk. 1, ch. 2.

decision about future action based on self-interest or future benefits. It was often used in the forum. *Epideictic* rhetoric seeks to persuade or educate the audience to hold or reaffirm a point of view in the present and is characterized by praise or blame. Its goal is a change of attitude or the deepening of values, and it was used in the marketplace or amphitheater.

The second element of rhetoric is *arrangement*, how a speech is structured. The *exordium* is the introduction of a speech. It states the purpose of the speech, focuses the attention of the audience, and gains their good will. The *narratio* gives the background facts for what will be discussed later. *Digressio* is a detour that gains the favor of the audience by giving them a break through a discussion of another related topic. The *propositio* is the thesis of the speech and states what the speaker wishes to prove. The *probatio* contains the proofs of the argument and appeals to the hearers' feelings and/or uses logical argument. The arguments are presented in the main body of the discourse called the *confirmatio*. This is supported by data from analogies, examples, or citations and may contain a *paraenesis* (moral exhortation) or a *refutation* (the alternative course presented in the worst possible way). Finally, the *peroratio* is the conclusion to the speech. This is when the speaker summarizes and gives alternatives to his or her argument, possibly by arousing the hearers' emotions.

The third element is *style*, which considers both the choice of words and their arrangement into sentences, including the use of appropriate figures of speech. Style is concerned with correctness, clarity, ornamentation, and propriety. *Memory*, the fourth element, consists of the preparation for natural delivery through memorization. And the last element is *delivery*, which governs the rules for control of the voice and the use of gestures appropriate for the occasion. Paul's letters show an author aware of these features.[8] He used whatever parts of ancient letter writing that fit the purpose ("rhetorical situation") of his particular letter.

---

8. Jerome Murphy-O'Connor, *Paul the Letter-Writer: His World, His Options, His Skills* (Collegeville, MN: Liturgical Press, 1995).

Organization, Dissemination, and Pauline Authorship of the Letters

Paul's letters are organized in two groups in the New Testament canon. The first group is written to churches (Romans through 2 Thessalonians) and the second group to individuals (1 and 2 Timothy, Titus, and Philemon). The letters can be further divided into those letters Paul wrote while in prison, the so-called Prison Epistles. First and Second Timothy and Titus are grouped together and called the Pastoral Epistles because they were written to two men who served as pastors of churches that had troubles with false teachers; Paul sent Timothy to Ephesus and Titus to the island of Crete. The earliest existent manuscripts of Ephesians lack the phrase "in Ephesus," which identifies the recipients' location (Eph. 1:1); this seeming omission suggests that Ephesians may have been a circular letter—that is, a letter intended for circulation among many churches. Galatians is likewise a circular letter intended for the "churches" in the area of Galatia (Gal. 1:2), which is modern Turkey.

One of the hotly debated issues among Pauline scholars is the authorship of the thirteen canonical letters. There is near universal agreement that Paul wrote Romans, 1 and 2 Corinthians, Galatians, Philippians, 1 Thessalonians, and Philemon. The "disputed" letters include Ephesians, Colossians, 2 Thessalonians, 1 and 2 Timothy, and Titus. Sometimes Hebrews is included as one of Paul's writings, but it is not considered part of the Pauline corpus, and most modern scholars do not accept its Pauline authorship. The issues related to this debate are complex and better treated when studying the letters individually. Suffice it to say, not all scholars are convinced that Paul did not write all the letters. There are good reasons to accept the traditional view that he was the primary source behind each letter. The questions and issues should not be quickly and naïvely glossed over, but after careful consideration, an informed decision is possible.

One of the appeals for the authenticity of the thirteen letters is that the differences can be accounted for because Paul used scribes called amanuenses to actually write down the letters (e.g., Tertius, Rom. 16:22). Writing materials were expensive, and so people often employed specialists to help them get their ideas written down. The debate is about how much freedom these scribes had in the writing process, such as choice of words. After the letter was written, the author would sign the letter with his own hand to verify the accuracy (1 Cor. 16:21; Gal. 6:11; Col. 4:18; 2 Thess. 3:17; Philem. v. 19). Although some of Paul's letters had coauthors, it is impossible to know how much they may have influenced the ideas or wording within the letters.

No original autographs of Paul's letters exist, only copied manuscripts. The oldest fragment of any of Paul's letters is P[46], one of the Chester Beatty Papyri discovered in an Egyptian graveyard in 1931 and dated to about AD 200. Textual critics study ancient manuscripts to reconstruct as close as possible what the reading of an original autograph may have been. From the second to the fourth centuries, Paul's letters were widely copied and circulated, and inevitably as a result, differences in manuscripts emerged. Many modern Bibles will provide a footnote of any significant differences in reading. There were seventeen different arrangements of the letters in various manuscripts of this period.[9]

By AD 397, the New Testament canon was universally accepted, including fourteen letters (with Hebrews) attributed to Paul. The order of the letters is generally in decreasing length and, as noted earlier, separated into two groups: letters to the churches and letters to individuals. Romans comes first because of its importance for Paul's theology. Chapter divisions were introduced into the Latin Vulgate by Stephen Langton at the beginning of the thirteenth century. Robert Stephanus further divided the Bible into verses in 1551.

---

9. Bruce M. Metzger, *The Canon of the New Testament: Its Origin, Development, and Significance* (Oxford, UK: Oxford University Press, 1987), 298.

Paul in His Social World

No one lives in a vacuum. We are all products of our own context and influenced to some degree by the social, religious, cultural, historical, and political contexts around us. To understand Paul and his letters, we need to learn the social language of the first-century Mediterranean world. Stowers writes, "Ancient letters will be difficult to understand on their own terms unless we also understand something about the contexts of Greco-Roman society in which the actions were performed and had their meanings."[10] Modern interpreters must recognize the many gaps that exist between Paul's world and ours. Somehow, we must build bridges from then to now in order to have a dialogue that leads to understanding.[11] Social-scientific criticism is the method modern interpreters use as a tool to build this bridge. One of the key aspects of this approach is to use "models" of typical behavior from the ancient world to help us understand not only the world behind the text but also the words actually written in the text.

A text has meaning only in a given social context. The world in which a person lives, or the world about which a person thinks or assumes, is socially constructed and created, and it is communicated and sustained through language and symbol. Language is never independent of its social context. The language of a text comes alive only in the mind of the reader when the reader shares a common social system with the writer or when the reader somehow learns about and engages in the type of thinking found in the original social system. Thus the intended meaning of a text can be understood only when one enters the social system of the original author and reader. The challenge we face with the New Testament, and Paul's letters in particular, is a lack of information about the earliest days

---

10. S. K. Stowers, *Letter Writing in Greco-Roman Antiquity* (Philadelphia: Westminster Press, 1986), 16.

11. John H. Elliott, *What Is Social-Scientific Criticism?* (Minneapolis: Fortress Press, 1993), 59.

of the church. That should caution us about being too dogmatic about any reconstruction of Paul's world or thought.

Monotheism and Polytheism

Social-scientific models look at the patterns of how people relate to one another and how they respond to their world. Paul and the earliest Christians increasingly came in conflict with their social world because of their new faith in Jesus Christ. This led to persecution, imprisonment, and even death. One significant type of conflict Paul and the early Christians experienced was their claim that "for us there is but one God, the Father, from whom all things came and for whom we live; and there is but one Lord, Jesus Christ, through whom all things came and through whom we live" (1 Cor. 8:6).

The chief characteristic of the religion in the first-century Roman Empire was syncretism. Syncretism is the "blending" of "elements of one religion with those of another."[12] Syncretism was a by-product of the shrinking Mediterranean world as travel became easier and cultures began to mix. Greek religion was characterized by polytheism, the worship of many gods. When the Romans conquered Greece and surrounding areas, they identified the Greek gods with their own and incorporated their own religions into the Greek religions. The cities of the Roman Empire were filled

> **Paul and the earliest Christians increasingly came in conflict with their social world because of their new faith in Jesus Christ.**

with temples and shrines to various gods and goddesses in the Roman-Greek pantheon. Idolatry was widespread and of every sort (Acts 17:16).

One of the most significant Roman religions of the time was the imperial ruler cult. This cult arose in Rome after Julius Caesar was assassinated in 44 BC, when an unpredicted comet appeared in July and was believed

12. David McEwan, "Syncretism, Religious," in *Global Wesleyan Dictionary of Theology*, ed. Al Truesdale (Kansas City: Beacon Hill Press of Kansas City, 2013), 521.

to have taken Caesar's soul to heaven. By vote of the Roman Senate and people, Julius was declared a god (Lat., *divus Julius* [divine Julius]). This made Octavian, later named Augustus, Julius's adopted son, a son of a god (Lat., *divi Julii filius* [son of divine Julius]). Augustus erected a temple for his deified father in 29 BC. Caligula (r. AD 37-41) was the first emperor to require worship of himself as a deity while he was still alive and punished anyone who did not worship him. A city could gain favor, protection, and economic benefits by bestowing honor on the emperor through this cult. The political value of the cult led to its obligatory, universal participation for the whole empire.

Another influential type of religion in many cities to which Paul traveled was known as the "mysteries." The mystery religions were private and public cults that had secret rites of initiation and rituals by which initiates received special, secret revelations. These mystery cults could be combined with the worship of various deities. The goal was to have an extraordinary experience of an immediate encounter or union with the divine. The initiation ceremonies used symbolic acts, visual effects, darkness, light, sacred objects, acts of purification, and rites of passage into a new life. At the basis of initiation was death and rebirth. There were also various forms of purification, sprinkling, or washing with water, but these were much different from Christian baptismal practices. Central to all mysteries was feasting or sharing in an opulent meal, often of sacrificed meat. The Eleusinian mysteries near Athens were the most famous. Another well-known cultic center worshipped the goddess Isis and was located near Cenchrea, close to Corinth. Paul used vocabulary similar to that of the mystery religions but filled these words with his own theology and focus upon Jesus Christ and the true "mystery" of God (Rom. 16:25; 1 Cor. 2:7; Eph. 3:4).[13]

---

13. See David A. Ackerman, *Transformation in Christ: Paul's Experience of the Divine Mystery* (Eugene, OR: Wipf and Stock, 2019).

Mixed into all of these religions was Judaism. After the Babylonian exile and the centuries that followed, Jews scattered all over the Mediterranean region. By the time of the first century, Judaism was an officially recognized religion, which allowed Jews to practice their faith openly. Most major cities had at least one Jewish synagogue where Jews met for prayer and instruction in the Scriptures. Scholars debate how different Hellenistic Judaism was from Palestinian Judaism. Many of the core elements were shared by both, but language and cultural influences created differences. There was diversity even within Palestinian Judaism, so it may be more accurate to use the plural "Judaisms."

Paul was fully aware of these religions and diligently called the new believers to "come out from them and be separate" (2 Cor. 6:17, quoting Isa. 52:11). The book of Acts shows how Paul used his encounters with the pagan cults and scattered Jews as opportunities to preach the gospel. His motive and method are summed up well in 1 Corinthians 9:22: "I have become all things to all people so that by all possible means I might save some."

Honor and Shame

The Mediterranean culture of Paul's day was significantly influenced by the value of honor. Honor presupposes some social norm, standard, or concept acceptable to a given group. Something that is accepted as honorable must be highly esteemed by the group. Shame results if a person or group fails to meet the test of honor, and so anything that causes shame must be avoided at great cost. Obligation and loyalty to a group could create cultural pressure to conform to preferred standards of honor. The pressure to conform to a group's standards influences the decisions people make and how they behave. Positions of honor in the ancient world were determined by power, gender, and social status. People were concerned about their reputations, social standings, and acceptance by the groups in which they placed their value and worth.[14]

Paul uses honor and shame throughout his letters to convince his readers to accept his ideas and conform to his ways. He is in the place of honor because of his association with Jesus Christ (1 Cor. 11:1), marked by his status as an apostle. He associated himself with the way of the cross, which is shameful to the world but represents the wisdom and power of God (1:23-24). His basic criterion for honor is spiritual maturity evidenced by a life of love, which results in union with Christ and fellowship in the community of faith. In the eyes of the world, Paul's way was shameful, weak, and to be rejected. He used rhetoric to shame his readers into abandoning their old ways, which were honorable and acceptable in their pagan environment but contrary to God's will of holiness (1 Thess. 4:3). Paul's call was to abandon worldliness and the way of the flesh and to be renewed in the image of Jesus Christ. The public reading of his letters created social pressure upon certain people to change (2 Thess. 3:14). The assumption in his letters is that because the readers believe in Jesus and have some sense of loyalty to Paul and one another, they will abandon their old life of sin and embrace the new life of holiness and love. The church becomes a new family of brothers and sisters, called "fictive kinship," united in one purpose and loyal to the gospel.

Patron and Client

First-century culture was characterized by the idea of "limited good"— that is, there are only so many assets available, and these assets must be divided among people. Inevitably, some will have more than others. Those of higher social status become the patrons, or those who possess more of the assets. As the power holders, patrons grant access to these assets to

---

14. Bruce J. Malina, *The New Testament World: Insights from Cultural Anthropology*, 3rd ed. (Louisville, KY: Westminster John Knox Press, 2001), 30.

others, who become the clients. This becomes a relationship of exchange in which each has something the other needs. It is asymmetrical because the parties are not equal in power. Inequality exists especially in possessing access to scarce material or spiritual resources. The client depends on the patron for either the provisions of the resources or the mediation to receive the provisions. This relationship by which resources are channeled to individuals or groups is particularistic and informal and is not meant to be bestowed universally. This relationship is subtle and not based on law but on understanding. It is often a binding and long-range relationship with a strong sense of interpersonal obligation. It is a voluntary relationship and can be abandoned at any time, although a client may have no choice but to ask the patron for help. Finally, it is a vertical relationship whereby a client is bound to one patron; "horizontal group organization and the solidarity of clients" are discouraged.[15]

Paul serves as the patron in his relationships with the churches. His "limited good" is the gospel and the correct interpretation of it. He is the patron of the divine mysteries (1 Cor. 2:1, 7; 4:1). He uses coercion through his strong rhetoric to encourage his readers to embrace his interpretation of the gospel as their own. According to Malina, a change based only on an abstract theological truth is of little value unless it includes challenging the honor, social standing, influence, or reputation of a person or group.[16] From Paul's perspective, the resolution of the conflict over spirituality must be one sided. He has the correct and only answer because his gospel came directly through revelation from Jesus Christ (Gal. 1:11-12). His interpretation will bring honor before God, but before the world, it may lead to shame experienced by suffering as Jesus did (Rom. 8:17).

15. John K. Chow, *Patronage and Power: A Study of Social Networks in Corinth*, Journal for the Study of the New Testament Supplement Series 75 (Sheffield, UK: JSOT Press, 1992), 31-32.

16. Bruce J. Malina, "Religion in the World of Paul," *Biblical Theology Bulletin* 16 (1986): 99.

Reading in Context

Although Paul's letters contain much theology, they speak to the real and pressing issues faced by the early church. The primary evidence we have of his thinking and worldview appears in the phraseology he used. Many things influenced his phraseology, including his upbringing, education, religious and cultural environment, and his own experiences of the resurrected and ever-present Jesus Christ. It is helpful to examine not only what Paul wrote but also how he wrote it. He obviously chose his words carefully and structured them so that his readers would be motivated to align their thinking with his. The more we can understand about Paul's world, the more accurately we can build a bridge to our own time. This will ensure that our interpretations are both faithful to Paul's intentions and applicable to our own needs. As we enter into his world, we will find that our own world is shaken, reevaluated, and transformed.

Because such a vast gulf exists between the reader of today and the world of the first century, we need to build bridges of understanding from *then* to *now*. Exploring the historical context of the author and original readers limits the possible meanings of a text and avoids the problem of imposing our own worldview upon the text. Words have particular meanings within a given historical context. If we want to know the meaning and purpose of Paul's words, we must do our best to enter into his world and under-

> **It is helpful to examine not only what Paul wrote but also how he wrote it.**

stand the limits of his language. There is a certain degree of timeless truth in all of Paul's letters. The problem we must avoid is confusing Paul's time-bound message to the early church with the timeless truth applicable to us. The following chapters will give some examples of how and why we must develop skills in this study of historical context and word usage.

Such careful study helps us not only distinguish the timeless from the time-bound but also understand the more confusing parts of Paul's letters. The end result will be a clearer and more biblical theology and a stronger basis for allowing Paul's letters to speak to a new generation.

2

Paul the Theologian

EPHESIANS 1:3-14

The interpretation process involves the crucial step of understanding the world behind the words on the page. Often readers use their imaginations to reconstruct this world. The problem is that their imaginations may not be accurate. They may be influenced more by their own worldviews than they are by the world of the text. The end result is that readers become the authorities that determine the meaning of the words. There are several outcomes when this happens. One is that there are as many meanings as there are interpreters. Another is that the meanings discovered may not be what the author intended, possibly even resulting in wrong doctrine.

The answer to this is to discover the world behind the text through understanding the historical context of the author. As Christian interpreters, we come to the Bible with the presupposition that God worked through the authors to relate an accurate and orthodox message. If we can discover the worldviews of the authors, we can then evaluate our own worldviews and make the necessary changes to ensure our thinking aligns with what God has said through the ancient text. This process involves several crucial steps. We can note the general worldviews of the time in question and then consider how or if these worldviews influenced the author. We can also consider the key aspects of the author's worldviews, specifically as they relate to God's purposes for humanity.

Major Worldviews of Paul's Day

All throughout his letters, Paul expects the readers to accept his ideas and conform to his way of thinking. He uses his persuasive rhetoric to accomplish this by including his own example and spiritual experiences, quotations from Scripture, established relationships, and logical argumentation. Another way to say this is that Paul wanted his readers to conform to his worldview. This raises the important question, what was Paul's worldview and what influenced it? A worldview or ideology can be defined as "the biases, opinions, preferences, and stereotypes of a particular writer and a particular reader. . . . A person's ideology concerns her or his conscious or unconscious enactment of presuppositions, dispositions, and values held in common with other people."[1] Ideology is influenced by relationships. "This integrated system proceeds from the need to understand, to interpret to self and others, to justify, and to control one's place in the world. Ideologies are shaped by specific views of reality shared by groups—specific perspectives on the world, society and man, and on the limitations and potentialities of human existence."[2]

One of the major debates in the twentieth century was over the background of and the influences upon Paul's thought. Was he influenced more by his Jewish background or his Hellenistic background? This question led interpreters to ask, What is at the center of his thought: Christology, anthropology, eschatology, apocalyptic, or ecclesiology? These questions are still highly debated and not easy to answer. A person doesn't have to study Paul's letters at some depth for very long before realizing that Paul used words employed by other religions. Did these religions influence his thinking in any way? At the end of the nineteenth and beginning of the

---

1. Vernon K. Robbins, *Exploring the Texture of Texts: A Guide to Socio-Rhetorical Interpretation* (Harrisburg, PA: Trinity Press International, 1996), 95.

2. John H. Elliott, *A Home for the Homeless: A Social-Scientific Criticism of 1 Peter, Its Situation and Strategy* (Minneapolis: Fortress Press, 1990), 268.

twentieth centuries, scholars in the "history of religions school" (Ger., *Religionsgeschichtliche Schüle*) contended that Paul's background could be traced to the Hellenistic religions of the period. In the latter part of the twentieth century, other scholars argued that Paul's background was more Jewish and that the only thing he had in common with the religions of his day was terminology.

The religious world of the first-century Roman Empire was quite diverse. Virtually everyone in the ancient world believed in some form of deity. Perhaps the most influential thinker was Plato (ca. 428–ca. 347 BC). By the time of Paul, Platonism had infiltrated the way of life of most of the Hellenistic world and may have influenced Judaism, as shown through the Jewish writer Philo of Alexandria (ca. 20 BC–ca. AD 50) and the Jewish wisdom and apocalyptic traditions. Platonism taught that the universe was created by a transcendent and immaterial God, sometimes called the demiurge. The highest attribute of God is the mind (*nous*) or reason (*logos*). God gave the human soul immortal reason. Lesser gods of the pantheon created the lesser parts of the universe and the human body.[3] The goal for humans is to cast off the flesh and enable the soul to discover truth and return to God, the ultimate Truth, Goodness, and Beauty.[4] Salvation involves escaping the bondage of the flesh, with the soul returning to God by discovering the truth through contemplation.[5] Intermediaries bridge the gulf between the human soul and the immortal God.

---

3. Plato, *The Timaeus of Plato*, secs. 40a, 41a-43a, trans. R. D. Archer-Hind (London: MacMillan, 1888), 130, 136-49, https://archive.org/details/timaeusofplato00platiala/page/n5/mode/2up.

4. Plato, *The Symposium*, secs. 210a-211e, trans. M. C. Howatson (Cambridge, UK: Cambridge University Press, 2008), 48-50, https://philarchive.org/archive/FREAR-4. Plato, *The Republic of Plato*, secs. 508-9, trans. A. D. Lindsay (London: J. M. Dent and Sons, 1923), 229-32, https://archive.org/details/therepublicofpla00platuoft/page/226/mode/2up.

5. Plato, *The Theaetetus of Plato*, sec. 176b, trans. S. W. Dyde (Glasgow: James MacLehose and Sons, 1899), 124-25, https://www.google.com/books/edition/The_Theaetetus_of_Plato/wt29k-Jz8pIC?hl=en&gbpv=1&dq. Plato, *Plato's Phaedo*, secs. 65e-66a, trans. F. J. Church (New York: Liberal Arts Press, 1951), 10-11, https://archive.org/details/PlatosPhaedo1954/page/n25/mode/2up.

These ideas were the foundation for what later became known as Gnosticism. Gnosticism was an eclectic religious system of different varieties based on the cosmological dualism of Platonism's flesh and soul, material and spiritual. Gnostics taught that Jesus was the intermediary between the transcendent God and the evil world. Jesus brought secret "knowledge" (*gnosis*) about human nature and how to be united with God. Since Jesus was from God, who is immaterial, Jesus only appeared to be human (a teaching known as Docetism). Salvation involved rejecting (asceticism) or ignoring (antinomianism)[6] the flesh. Some Pauline scholars of the early to mid-twentieth century argued that Paul was influenced by Gnosticism (Walter Schmithals, Rudolf Bultmann). However, more recent scholars have clarified this claim and shown that the New Testament recounts only the beginnings of Gnosticism in the early church. Over the next century following the New Testament period, Gnosticism developed until it became a major heresy challenging the church.

The mystery religions are also often compared to Paul's thinking. Some of Paul's converts, particularly those in Corinth, may have come out of the mysteries or were at least influenced by them. The mysteries were syncretistic and included elements from other religions. Salvation in the mysteries was experienced through secret initiation ceremonies. These ceremonies, often performed at night, symbolized a change of mind—a transformation—through an experience with the sacred. This charismatic experience was in effect a reenactment of a cultic community's foundational myth. The initiation was in essence a representation of death and rebirth.

Included in the ceremonies were different forms of purification, sprinkling, or washing with water, but these rites differed considerably from

---

6. "Antinomianism" is a term derived from two Greek words for "against" and "law." Thus the term refers to the rejection of socially established morality or moral law. For this type of Gnosticism, if the flesh or body is considered evil and the spirit good, then one's behavior is of no concern, since it only involves the physical body.

Christian baptismal practices. Humiliation, pain, psychological terror, and serious injuries were also common during initiation. Other features of the mysteries included visionary experiences, ecstatic utterances, fasting, beating of drums, and ringing of cymbals. The cult of Mithras performed the ritual slaughter of a bull as a divine sacrifice, with the blood of the bull giving life. The ritual included bread and a cup of water and employed an image of resurrection. Not all of these practices were universal, and the theologies were not consistent.

Although there are notable similarities between Paul's theology and the practices of the early church, and the theologies and practices of the religions he encountered in his travels, the core ideas are clearly different. Paul may have purposely used the religious terms of his opponents and redefined them according to his own theology. He used words and concepts to help his converts understand that Jesus is the true wisdom (1 Cor. 1:25), knowledge (8:1), and revelation of the mystery of God (2:6-8; Rom. 16:25; Eph. 3:3-4).

God's Plan for Us *in Christ*

Paul's exclusive claim of "one God" and "one Lord" came in conflict with the pluralism of the religions around him (1 Cor. 8:5-6). He believed that the gospel of Jesus Christ is the fulfillment of the Jewish faith, and he quotes the Old Testament numerous times in his letters to support this idea (see ch. 5, "Paul's Hermeneutical Method"). Christianity was not a new religion; rather, it was planned before creation and was the continuation of God's promise to Abraham. Like other religious systems, Paul believed that God is immortal but became incarnated and present on earth in Jesus Christ. God's love is most profoundly revealed in the death and resurrection of Jesus Christ. God continues to dwell with people through the Holy Spirit.

Paul should not be isolated from his socioreligious environment and could have been indirectly influenced from any number of directions. However, his ideology is expressed through the filter of his concern for his churches. His ideology is always given from his own perspective and is veiled behind his guidance for specific situations faced by the early church.[7] As a Pharisee, he was steeped in first-century Judaism, yet he recognized that his message needed to be understood by both Jews and Gentiles (1 Cor. 9:19-23). Therefore, he picked terms and images that were relevant to the situations at hand. Although he was willing to contextualize the gospel for the Hellenistic environs of his churches, he did not want to distort the gospel's basic message.[8] The primary influence on his ideology was his theology. At the core of his contextualization was the "Christ event" of the death and resurrection of Jesus Christ. His experience of the risen Jesus Christ through the presence and power of the Holy Spirit was the well from which he drew his ideas to manage the situations in the churches. As interpreters, we must piece together Paul's thought from the contextualized application of it found throughout his various letters.

At the heart of Paul's thought lies the *kerygma* (Gk., "proclamation") of Jesus Christ. This message involved more than knowing *about* Jesus the Messiah. Jesus was more than a person to be studied and admired—he was a power to be experienced. Simply stated, for Paul, the goal of human existence is fellowship with God in Christ through the Holy Spirit. Paul expresses this idea in many ways, but one particular phrase is highly revealing of his thinking. He uses the prepositional phrase "in Christ" over 161 times in its various forms, including pronouns. Other prepositions are also

---

7. Johan Christiann Beker, *Paul the Apostle: The Triumph of God in Life and Thought* (Philadelphia: Fortress Press, 1980), 11.

8. Dean Flemming, "Essence and Adaptation: Contextualization and the Heart of Paul's Gospel" (PhD diss., University of Aberdeen, 1987), 102, 533.

used with "Christ" to express the special bond believers have with Christ, including "with Christ," "of Christ," and "Christ in you." The technical construction "in Christ" is called in Greek grammar a locative of sphere, using the dative case preceded (in most instances) with the preposition "in" (*en*). This is an illustrative way of describing the "place" or realm in which a person exists. This new existence influences every aspect of who we are and enables us to be new creations (2 Cor. 5:17).

We cannot enter this new existence by human meditation, intellect, or effort, but only by faith that willingly receives God's love and grace shown through Jesus's death and resurrection. This is a reciprocal relationship—that is, us in Christ and Christ in us (Col. 1:27). This new existence is described in different ways in Paul's letters, depending on the purpose, situation, and audience. Critical to this idea is sovereignty: who or what will be the primary determiner of the direction, thought, and lifestyle of a person. There are two alternatives for Paul: either sin is in control or Christ is in control. Paul describes these two alternatives in many different ways.

All people are born into the fallen condition of sin. Paul traces this back to the decision of self-sovereignty made by Adam when he and Eve ate the forbidden fruit from the Tree of the Knowledge of Good and Evil in Genesis 3. All people inherit the consequences of this decision and are born "in Adam." Being a descendant of Adam does not in and of itself make us guilty of sin before God but only destines us for death (Rom. 5:12; 1 Cor. 15:21-22). The more serious problem is when we allow our weakened nature to reject God's sovereignty by disobeying God's laws (Rom. 3:23; 6:23). We follow in the same path as Adam in our rebellion against God, most vividly expressed as disobedience and pride. Disobedience shows up in depravity and wicked behaviors (1:28-32). Pride shows up in religious arrogance and legalism (2:1, 17-24). God responds to disobedience and pride with judgment and wrath (1:18; 2:5). Sin becomes particularly evident in the yearning to please instincts and desires that have become distorted by selfishness. Paul calls this living "in the flesh" (see 8:5-9, ESV; Gal. 5:19-21). The ideology of the world is controlled by sin and the flesh, leading people into a bondage from which they cannot escape without God's gracious intervention in Christ (Rom. 6:14; 7:21-25).

Paul's basic message is consistent throughout his letters: the only solution to this problem of sin is Jesus Christ. First and foremost, the war with sin and its consequence of death has already been won through Jesus's resurrection from the dead (1 Cor. 15:56-57). Jesus's death upon the cross served as a sacrifice of atonement, removing the penalty for sins committed in rebellion against God. The result is the offer of justification and removal of guilt for all who trust in this gracious offer of forgiveness (Rom. 3:23-25). The efficacy of Jesus's death was then verified by his resurrection from the dead (4:25). His resurrection showed his power over the deep heart issue of the power of sin. His resurrection provides the resource to bring new life free from the control of sin to those who come in faith to receive this gift.

Paul systematically presents these ideas in Romans 6–8, although the basic themes are found in many other places. Romans 6:4 gives a summary of how a person moves from the realm of sin to the realm of Christ: "We were buried therefore with him by baptism into death, in order that, just as Christ was raised from the dead by the glory of the Father, we too might walk in newness of life" (ESV). One becomes a participant in this existence by identifying with Christ's death and resurrection through dying to the old way of life controlled by sin and rising to the new way of life controlled by righteousness. Dying, being buried, putting off the old self (Eph. 4:22), being crucified with Christ (Gal. 2:20), and other similar images basically describe the essential change of allegiance that must take place to find freedom from sin. Death to the old self symbolizes the cessation of relationship. Every thought, word, and deed must now come under the control of Christ. We allow Christ to be the new power for life (Phil. 1:21) by yielding ourselves in total commitment and faith. No longer do we trust our own efforts (spiritual pride) or seek to please ourselves (living by the flesh), but we trust in Jesus as Lord supreme. The act of baptism symbolizes the change from the old to the new. Being "in Christ" brings freedom from sin and freedom for new life. Paul realized the futility of living to please his own desires (3:4-11). He had to come to the point of being crucified with Christ (Gal. 2:20) by dying to the old life. The crucified life becomes the source for victory from sin's control (6:14). When the hold of sin is broken in our lives, we now have the divine resources to overcome temptations (1 Cor. 10:13) and the acts of sin (Rom. 6:15).

This new life is characterized by transformation into the likeness of Christ (2 Cor. 3:18). We experience new creation as we change the focus of our devotion from the objects of the world to the person of Christ. The deep inner change that happens as we accept in faith God's grace comes through the Holy Spirit, who renews our thinking (Rom. 8:5-7) and teaches us the "mind of Christ" (1 Cor. 2:16). The mind represents the deep inner person where decisions are made. The Holy Spirit helps us develop our conscience, which serves as the guide for our behavior and thinking. This is experienced as the "fruit of the Spirit," of which love is primary (Gal. 5:22-23). The basic requirement for this transformation is to "walk in step with the Spirit" (v. 25, BSB) through the obedience of faith. The final result of this process of sanctification is eternal life (Rom. 6:22). To be "in Christ" is to be fully committed to his supremacy in our lives and to be in full surrender to the guidance of

> **To be "in Christ" is to be fully committed to his supremacy in our lives and to be in full surrender to the guidance of the Holy Spirit.**

the Holy Spirit. This profound relationship opens the floodgates of God's grace and enables us to experience all that God has planned for us.

Created to Be *in Christ*

The inductive method of interpretation seeks to allow each passage to speak on its own terms. Conclusions are arrived at after careful interpretation of the historical and literary contexts and various details of the passage. One value of this approach is that it functions as a test and clarification for any broader conclusions, such as those given in the previous section. Every passage in Paul's letters must be interpreted as its own moment in communication. Drawing upon the literary and historical contexts refines, clarifies, and focuses this message so that the particular purpose is not lost or confused. In this way, particular passages, chapters, and letters take on their own characteristics. As these characteristics are combined with other passages that have gone through a similar process, overarching themes begin to emerge. It becomes helpful to cross-link the ideas of one passage to those found in another, not to proof-text a particular interpretation, but to clarify and develop our understanding of Paul's overall ideology. This approach is foundational for developing an accurate biblical theology and application to modern contexts.

Many years of study have convinced me that the theological orientation of being *in Christ* stands behind each of Paul's letters and guides his specific application of the gospel to the local issues of the churches. A thorough investigation of Paul's *in Christ* ideology and verification of this thesis would require an extensive study of each of his letters.[9] This is what books on Paul's theology attempt to do. Another approach would be to find a representative passage that in our best judgment contains many of the key elements of Paul's thinking. Ephesians 1:3-14 is such a passage and

9. See Ackerman, *Transformation in Christ*.

provides an open window into many of the key ideas that motivated Paul's ministry and letter writing.

There are several reasons why Ephesians 1:3-14 is a useful passage for this purpose. First, there is a concentration of eleven uses of the phrase "in Christ" and its variations. The repeated use of such a phrase suggests what is important to the author. Second, often the opening of the body of a letter contains a summary of the key ideas to be dealt with later on. In the case of Ephesians, this passage sets the theological foundation for everything else written in the letter. Ephesians 1–4 represents one of the most concise statements of Paul's theology, and so the introduction to these chapters offers a summary of this theology. Third, the long sentence structure (one long sentence of 204 words in the Greek) suggests that Paul (the assumed author) intentionally structured his language to make a significant statement in the most concise and impactful way. English translations often divide this section into smaller units to make it easier for modern readers.

Ephesians 1:3 marks the beginning of the body of the letter and is given in the form of a blessing and praise to "the God and Father of our Lord Jesus Christ." Paul extends his ideas throughout this long sentence by using relative clauses that give reasons for praising God. The word "blessing" is repeated three times in this opening verse. Paul praises God for the spiritual blessings found "in Christ." In these verses, Paul lists seven blessings that God gives believers who are *in Christ*: election (v. 4), adoption (v 5), redemption and forgiveness (v. 7), revelation (vv. 8-9), the Holy Spirit (v. 13), and future redemption (v. 14).[10]

These blessings are "spiritual" because they are mediated by the Holy Spirit (v. 13).[11] These blessings are linked to Christ in various prepositional

---

10. George Lyons, Robert W. Smith, and Kara Lyons-Pardue, *Ephesians/Colossians/Philemon*, New Beacon Bible Commentary (Kansas City: Beacon Hill Press of Kansas City, 2019), 48.

11. Andrew T. Lincoln, *Ephesians*, Word Biblical Commentary 42 (Dallas: Word Books, 1990), 20-21.

phrases: "in Christ" (v. 3); "in him" (vv. 4, 9, 10); "in [the] Christ" (vv. 10, 12); "before him" (v. 4); "through Jesus Christ" (v. 5); "into him" (v. 5); "in the Beloved" (v. 6); "in whom" (vv. 7, 11, and twice in v. 13) (AT). "In Christ" and its variations show the source by which God brings these blessings and the new existence that results from the salvation brought by Jesus's death and resurrection. The repeated focus on Christ gives this passage the quality of a hymn.

This new life in Christ has been God's plan "before the foundation of the world" (v. 4, NASB). It was not God's plan B but has always been plan A. The very reason God spoke creation into existence was so that humanity could be "holy and blameless . . . in love" in Christ (v. 4, NKJV). These are essential qualities of God and are experienced most fully through Christ (4:24; 5:1-2). Jesus's death and resurrection were not the solution to the problem of sin that God thought up after Adam and Eve's disobedience but were the plan from the beginning of time (2 Tim. 1:9-10; 1 Pet. 1:19-20; Rev. 13:8). God's plan of salvation is based on God's love and grace and not as a response to sin or the self-righteous efforts of humanity.

God's sovereignty is never in doubt in any of Paul's letters. God's sovereignty can be experienced by people as grace or judgment. This letter offers the readers the opportunity to experience God's grace through faith (Eph. 2:8-9). God's grace can be seen in how God predestined that his grace would be experienced in Christ (v. 5). "To predestine" means "to decide or purpose beforehand."[12] God planned how salvation would be experienced and not the individuals who would participate in this salvation. In other words, Christ is the one who is predestined as the way to new life. The invitation is open to all people, but unfortunately many are blinded by sin and deceived by the enemy (vv. 1-2). God's will is for

---

12. Walter Bauer, Frederick W. Danker, W. F. Arndt, and F. Wilbur Gingrich, *A Greek-English Lexicon of the New Testament and Other Early Christian Literature*, 3rd ed. (Chicago: University of Chicago Press, 2000), 873.

everyone to experience holiness and love in Christ (5:27; Col. 1:22; 1 Thess. 4:3; 1 Tim. 2:4; 2 Pet. 3:9). God desires all to be saved but will not override the necessary response of faith and love.

The specific goal of God's plan is for all people to be adopted into his new family (Eph. 1:5). Adoption was a common practice in Paul's time that granted the same privileges as the children naturally born. Paul uses the image of adoption to express the new identity of those who are in Christ. This adoption happens "through Jesus Christ" (v. 5) and is experienced through the work of the Holy Spirit (Rom. 8:15). This family finds its identity in acknowledging Christ's supremacy. He is the "head" of this new family called the "church" (Eph. 1:22; 4:15; 5:23).

Ephesians 1:6 finally expresses why God has planned this adoption: so that we may know the depth of God's grace that comes through "the Beloved," referring to Christ (NASB). There is no better way to know what God's grace is than to experience the new life found in Christ. A good definition of grace is that God took the initiative in all this, since it was God's plan and not our searching for the transcendent God through our own efforts, good works, rituals, or obedience to the law. All of these are worthless expressions of pride and only bring further bondage (2:8-9). Both Gentiles in all of their various religions and Jews in their prideful traditions have been deceived into thinking that salvation can be found through human effort. God's plan in Christ shows that salvation is all about God's offer of grace. This grace is glorious because it opens the way for humanity to be restored to the image of God so that we can experience full reconciliation with our Creator (Rom. 3:23; 2 Cor. 3:18).

This adoption is made possible because of the redemption that comes through Jesus's sacrificial death on the cross (Eph. 1:7). "Redemption" means "to buy" or "to purchase," for example, a slave in bondage.[13]

---

13. Ibid., 117.

Through his death, Jesus redeemed those cursed by the condemnation of the law and trapped by sin (Gal. 3:13; 4:5). We experience redemption by the forgiveness of our sins ("trespasses," Rom. 5:15-17; 2 Cor. 5:19; Eph. 2:5; Col. 1:14). As we are freed from the bondage and condemnation of sin, we begin to experience the purifying work of the Holy Spirit (Titus 2:14). Again, this is all a matter of grace. From the world's perspective, this plan of salvation is foolish, but it actually shows how glorious, gracious, and wise God is (Eph. 1:8; 1 Cor. 1:18-25). Paul goes one step further and claims that this plan of redemption includes all creation, "things in the heavens and things on the earth" (Eph. 1:10, NASB). This reveals Paul's eschatology (see ch. 9, "Eschatology"). What Christ did at a certain point in time culminates and reveals God's mysterious plan and will bring about the restoration of all creation to God's purposes for it (Rom. 8:21-22). God's plan was made *in Christ*, was fulfilled *in Christ*, and is experienced by those who are *in Christ*.

This gift of glorious grace is so overwhelming that it is beyond words. This gift is not deserved but must be received in faith to experience its desired goal (Rom. 3:22, 25-26; Gal. 2:16). The goal of grace is reconciliation with God through communion with the resurrected Jesus, who is experienced in this life through the indwelling Holy Spirit. Grace is the primary experience of God's presence in this life that brings victory over the power of sin and the temptation to commit the acts of sin (Rom. 6:14-15). Grace requires the response of faith for it to bring salvation. Faith allows grace to produce in us the fruit of good works (Eph. 2:10).

Paul's language of the gospel as the "mystery" of God may echo some of the religions of his day, but his meaning is much different. The word "mystery" in Ephesians 1:9 refers to something hidden or secret that must be revealed to be known. Paul defines God's mystery as his purpose set forth in Christ. The mystery of God's plan was for the Beloved Son to come one day and redeem humanity. This was hidden from creation, though seen in part by the prophets of Israel (Rom. 16:25-26; Eph. 3:9). Paul was given special insight into this mystery through his experience of the resurrected Christ (Eph. 3:3-4). The mystery of God's plan is inclusive of all creation when "all things in heaven and on earth" will be united in Christ (1:10). This mystery is experienced vividly now through the church, especially in the way Jews and Gentiles become one people under the lordship of Christ (3:6; Col. 1:26-27). A Christian believer, unlike an adherent of a mystery religion, does not need to go through any special initiation ceremony to participate in the mystery of Christ. Paul did not want baptism to be viewed as the initiation rite of any self-proclaimed spiritually elite (see 1 Cor. 1:14-17). Christian baptism is the outward testimony that represents the inner decision of faith to die to the old way of life and experience the new life in Christ (Rom. 6:4).

In Ephesians 1:11, Paul again points out that God took the initiative in this plan and predestined it all according to his purpose. When persons enter into the new existence of being in Christ, they are privileged as adopted children to participate in God's eternal plan of redemption. The difficult passive verb *eklērōthēmen* ("chosen," NIV) possesses the connotation of destiny. The destiny of every human is to be found in Christ. Sadly, many people choose to remain trapped by sin and self and never get to enjoy God's plan for them. God's plan for our adoption in Christ entitles us to receive an inheritance guaranteed by the Holy Spirit (v. 14). God's sovereignty is the source of this plan, which guarantees that the plan will happen and guarantees the inheritance will be given. This inheritance is implied in the purpose clause of v. 12: "so that we who were the first to hope in Christ might be to the praise of his glory" (ESV). God's plan is sure, and so the salvation of those in Christ is also guaranteed. The security of the believer comes not from the side of faith but from the side of grace. The required human decision of faith can be seen in the word "first to hope" (*proēlpikotas*). Faith in Christ is the prerequisite for the power of this grace to become operative. Paul may be reflecting on the first generation of Christians who passed on this hope to the next generation—namely, the people like the Ephesians (v. 13). It is through this entire plan of redemption that God will be seen for who he is: loving, gracious, and holy. That all things exist in and for Christ serves the purpose of letting God's glory be seen through all creation (v. 12).

The object of our hope is Christ. The one through whom we receive redemption is Christ. The one in whom the Holy Spirit sanctifies is Christ. The key to move from the realm of sin to the realm of Christ is to hear the "word of truth" and believe in Christ (v. 13). Faith is the open door. This faith is not simply intellectual but all-encompassing conse-cration as we lay ourselves before Christ and allow him to be sovereign. The Holy Spirit makes this transition real for each believer in the present moment and instills a deepening desire to experience the fullness of Christ in the age to come (v. 10). Returning to verse 4, we now see that being in Christ is the only route to experience God's purpose for us to be holy and loving.

> **That all things exist in and for Christ serves the purpose of letting God's glory be seen through all creation.**

The Call to Newness Today

Passages such as this one in Ephesians should leave us as readers hungering for what Paul writes about and celebrating that it is a real possibility in our lives. This life of holiness in Christ is not for certain people who go through a special initiation process, as in some of the pagan religious practices of Paul's day. Sadly, even people in our day seek holiness through efforts not too different from Platonism, Gnosticism, or the mystery religions. These terms are not generally used, but the ideologies are found everywhere. Even empty religious practices, such as those of the Jews of Paul's day, feed the pride of people, who then come to think that being good enough will somehow win them eternal life.

Our theological presuppositions are power ploys in our effort to hear the ancient words of the Bible. It would not be difficult to slip into the defense of certain theological positions when reading a Scripture passage. There is strong language in Ephesians 1:3-14 about such cherished doctrines as predestination, election, and grace. We must ask, is Paul's goal here to lay out a systematic theology of grace or to argue for the predestination of certain individuals? The more I study this passage, the more I have come to believe that this passage primarily gives us a view into Paul's deep thinking about who Christ is and what God has done in and through Christ on our behalf. Paul's ideology is clearly Christocentric, but this ideology is bound to his broader theology of who God is and what God as creator of the universe desires for his creation. Paul's Christology points to his theology. What merges these two is our real-life experience through the Holy Spirit.

As readers, we are left with the challenge of our own worldviews and how our ideology has been so colored and even warped by the world that we cannot see God's plan if we remain stuck in this ideology. As descendants of Adam (and Eve), we are trapped by sin and death, unable to rescue ourselves from this curse. Everything we do seems to somehow come back to self-preservation, creature comforts, distorted desires, and warped philosophies. These are the effects of being enslaved to sin.

A simple reading of this passage may shake us a little. A repeated and deep study may move us off of our comfortable foundations. We may find that our old ways of thinking are not sufficient anymore. The hope about which Paul writes here is what our hearts deeply long for. Why? Because that is the very reason we have been created.

We would be wise to evaluate all that influences our thinking. How has our ideology been shaped by our culture, our family upbringing, our choices in life, and the activities in which we have participated? Not all of these will be bad or sinful, but they will be part of this world. God calls us to something greater that transcends all of these while transforming them into God's purposes for us. This is the basic idea found in the well-known passage of Romans 12:1-2. The transformation and renewing of the mind about which Paul writes in that text can happen only as a person has moved over to the new realm of Christ's lordship. The fully sanctified life is willing to be molded by the power and guidance of the Holy Spirit. The most important decision a person can make in life is what to do with Jesus.

3

The Personal Letter

PHILEMON

Writing a Personal Letter

Paul kept in contact with the churches he started or planned to visit by writing letters. These letters were often sent by couriers who were part of his ministry team. Over a hundred years ago, German scholar Adolf Deissmann studied ancient papyri and noted a difference between an "epistle" (more of a literary essay) and a "letter" (personal communication).[1] Deissmann's conclusions have since been challenged, but he set the direction for much research on the styles and forms of Paul's letters known as epistolography. Epistolography examines the genre of a letter in order to find appropriate and useful ways to interpret it. The research on this topic has expanded significantly and has proven helpful for interpreting difficult passages in Paul's letters.

Paul wrote his letters both to individuals and churches. Even the letters written to individuals (1 and 2 Timothy, Titus, and Philemon) have a community, such as a house church, as the implied audience. Paul's letters were meant to be read out loud and publicly to many people (Col. 4:16; 1 Thess. 5:27). In the honor-shame culture of that time, this may have put social pressure upon individuals within the church to conform to Paul's directions. Philemon, the shortest of Paul's canonical letters, may have had

---

1. G. Adolf Deissmann, *Bible Studies*, trans. Alexander Grieve (Edinburgh: T. and T. Clark, 1901).

this purpose. Its small size and relegation to the end of the Pauline corpus often lead people to neglect a close reading of it, and so they miss out on its message for a new day. Because of its small size, it can serve as a useful example for studying other letters of Paul. Knowledge and skills learned in studying Philemon can be applied to longer letters.

Letters capture a moment of dialogue between two parties. In the ancient world, letters were a way of communicating over long distances. There were many types of letters at that time. The most common was the personal letter, which was sent to family and friends. The basic format of this type of letter did not change from the third century BC to the third century AD. The language of personal letters showed familiarity and used relational and personal terms.[2] Philemon is a personal letter and the short-est of any of Paul's letters, with 335 words, though this would be considered a long private letter in the Greco-Roman world.

> **In the ancient world, letters were a way of communicating over long distances.**

Letters in the ancient world, like many letters today, followed a certain basic structure, with an opening, body, and conclusion (see ch. 1, "Paul's Mission to the World"). A simple illustration can be found in Claudius's letter to Felix in Acts 23:26-30, when Paul was transferred to Caesarea for further trial (although this letter apparently lacks a well-defined closing). Each of these parts can be further divided. Paul's letters have many of the same elements as other letters of his time but are much longer. He did not write in isolation but was trained to some degree in the letter-writing principles of his day. He was probably less concerned about fitting his writing to any set pattern than he was about communicating his message. Therefore, he used whatever literary forms were common in his day to accomplish this. He could use, expand, or disregard any form according to his purpose.

---

2. David E. Aune, *The New Testament in Its Literary Environment* (Philadelphia: Westminster Press, 1987), 162.

A number of background questions can be asked of a letter: Who wrote it and to whom was it sent? Why was it written? Were there any background issues that prompted the author to write this letter (called the "rhetorical situation")? For purposes of this chapter, we will look at two types of questions: historical and literary. Looking at what can be known about the historical background helps us understand the context from which and for which Paul wrote a letter. Building upon the historical background helps us be more precise in our interpretation of Paul's method of communication and intended message. All of this helps us arrive at our ultimate question: What is the relevance of this letter for us today?

Philemon shows some similarities to Paul's letter to the Colossians. Philemon, the recipient, may have lived in or near Colossae, which suggests that Paul wrote both letters about the same time and from the same place. Colossians also shares many similarities with Ephesians, which makes the provenance of the letters more challenging to figure out. Looking into the background of Colossians helps us narrow our search for the background of Philemon. Colossae was located along the Lycus River in Phrygia, along the main road from the East to Ephesus. It shared the same fertile and rich valley as Laodicea. There is no clear record of when this church started, but it possibly began during Paul's almost three-year ministry in Ephesus, as recounted in Acts 19 (see v. 10).

Paul is in prison as he writes both letters (Philem. vv. 1, 9; Col. 4:3, 10, 18). The question is, Where was he imprisoned at this time? He was in prison in many places, but the two primary choices for these letters are Ephesus and Rome. The answer to this issue impacts the dating of the letter. In verse 22 of Philemon, Paul asks Philemon to prepare him a guest room. This indicates that Paul expected to be released from prison and to visit Colossae soon (or this could have been merely wishful thinking). Colossae was about one hundred miles from Ephesus. Ephesus would have been the closest major city for Onesimus to flee. Rome was over one thousand miles away, which creates questions of feasibility. How likely would it have been for Onesimus to be there and also for Paul to visit Philemon? One significant problem with an Ephesian imprisonment is the absence of any mention of it in Acts or Paul's letters, although not all of Paul's imprisonments are mentioned in the New Testament. Paul may have hoped for a release from his Roman imprisonment and planned another missionary journey eastward to visit the churches. Little is known about his Roman imprisonment except the brief description of his house arrest at the end of Acts 28. At least early on, he had relative freedom under house arrest to accept visitors. His Roman imprisonment was in the early AD 60s. The problem of dating and location cannot be solved, but it is helpful to have the general idea of Paul's circumstances when writing the letter.

In support of Colossae being Onesimus's home and of Philemon living in or near this city is the mention of many of the same names in the letter to the Colossians and the letter to Philemon. This presupposes that the two letters were written around the same time and sent more or less to the same place. Paul mentions five people in verse 23 of Philemon whom the Colossians knew: Epaphras (Col. 4:12), Mark (v. 10), Aristarchus (v. 10), Demas (v. 14), and Luke (v. 14). Archippus is also mentioned in both letters (Philem. v. 2; Col. 4:17). Demas, Mark, and Luke are mentioned in 2 Timothy 4:10-11, indicating that they were with Paul at some point when he wrote that letter. The assumption has been that Paul was imprisoned in Rome when he wrote his second letter to Timothy. Colossians 4:7-9 also indicates that Onesimus would be returning to Colossae with Tychicus. In 2 Timothy 4:12, Paul sent Tychicus to Ephesus (see Eph. 6:21), although it would have been an easy trip for him to continue on to Colossae after visiting Timothy, who was stationed in Ephesus. Letters at that time had to be hand delivered by special couriers representing the sender. Tychicus could have carried all three letters with him back to Asia Minor. The above evidence leans toward Paul being imprisoned in Rome, where somehow he had met Onesimus. These ideas are far from conclusive but at least offer a possible historical setting to the letter.

The key topic of the letter to Philemon can be determined from within the letter itself. The basic issue is that Paul wants Philemon to accept Onesimus back as a brother. The letter focuses upon the possible outcome for Onesimus, who had become a believer after he met Paul (v. 10). The traditional view is that Onesimus had run away as a slave from Philemon and had somehow become acquainted with Paul. There is no indication of when or under what circumstances the two met, but it was obviously providential. Under Paul's evangelism, Onesimus had become a believer (v. 10). He may have known of Paul when Paul had visited Colossae and so had initially been exposed to the gospel in this setting. When he met Paul, who was still imprisoned, he may have seen in Paul a friend and advocate for his situation. An alternative view is that the Colossian church, specifically Philemon, had sent Onesimus to check on Paul's condition in Rome. If this was the case, Onesimus did not want to return because of the freedom he had experienced through this journey. Paul needed to check on the situation in Colossae and the Lycus Valley, and so he took the opportunity to send Onesimus back as a new person. The case for the traditional view is stronger and more widely accepted today.

This raises the important historical issue of slavery in the Roman Empire. A significant portion of the population of the Roman Empire consisted of slaves, up to 90 percent in some major cities. Slavery was a social institution throughout the empire; no province was untouched. It was part of everyday life, even for early Christians (see 1 Cor. 7:21-23; Gal. 3:28; Eph. 6:5-8; Col. 3:11, 22; 1 Tim. 6:1-2; Titus 2:9). Persons became slaves through conquest, economic hardship, or birth. Slaves were the workforce of the empire and had a wide range of jobs, from working in mines or laboring on farms to running some of the finest households in the empire. Some were well-educated and served as teachers and writers. Some became part of the *familia* and were entrusted with important jobs, even raising children. Slaves had some rights; for example, they could marry, earn money, and even purchase their own freedom in some situations. This possibility of freedom served as a motivation for obedience and hard work. For the most part, however, slavery in the Roman Empire was oppressive and difficult. Running away was a strong temptation. If caught, the punishment could be brutal, even death.

There is no indication of what type of slave Onesimus was or what job he had in Philemon's household. The typical household of modest size would have slaves who did all the domestic chores and farmwork. Since the Lycus Valley is fertile, Philemon may have been involved in agriculture or a related business. The letter implies that Onesimus, at some point, had gone away and not returned. The traditional assumption is that he had stolen something and ran away, although this is reading between the lines of the letter. There is also no way to know how Onesimus met Paul. The letter simply asks for Philemon to accept Onesimus back without punishing him, which the law allowed. If we listen carefully, even with a bit of guided imagination, we can eavesdrop into a conversation about grace and restoration.

An Impassioned Call for Freedom

Opening (Philem. vv. 1-3)

Some of Paul's letters have extended openings (Rom. 1:1-7; Gal. 1:1-5; Titus 1:1-4). Although the opening of Philemon is rather short, there are important hints at the themes that will be taken up later.

1. *Author (Philem. v. 1a)*

The salutation indicates that this letter was coauthored by Paul and Timothy. Paul usually includes some self-description with his name in his letters (except 1 and 2 Thessalonians). He does not appeal to his apostolic authority in this letter. Instead, he references his humbled condition as "a prisoner of Christ Jesus" (see 2 Tim. 1:8). This description suggests that he was in prison because of his faith in Christ. The Roman authorities may have thought they had Paul under lock and key, but he was actually free because of the transforming power of Jesus Christ. Prison bars and shackles could not keep Paul's voice silent as he shared the gospel with his prison guards and fellow prisoners and wrote letters.

Roman prisons were notorious for being places of cruelty. If Paul wrote this letter during his house arrest described in Acts 28, he may have had some degree of freedom. At least we know that he had Timothy with him at this time. Additional names associated with his Roman imprisonment (and other imprisonments) indicate that other Christians checked on him and cared for his needs (Phil. 2:19-30). Knowing something of the historical setting can help us reconstruct the situation from which Paul wrote and also how he may have met Onesimus.

Besides the letter to Philemon, Timothy is mentioned as the coauthor in a number of Paul's letters (2 Corinthians, Philippians, Colossians, 1 and 2 Thessalonians), especially the Prison Epistles. Timothy was Paul's closest missionary companion. He was with Paul during the mission in Ephesus (Acts 19:22), and so it is likely that the Colossians knew him, which is why Paul calls him "our brother" (Philem. v.1). "Brother" is a term of fictive kinship that developed in the early church and shows the close family bond believers experienced together. Timothy was a key leader in the early church. The first time he is mentioned is in Acts 16:1-2, when Paul met him on his second missionary trip through the area of Lystra, a

Lycaonian town in the Roman province of Galatia. Paul saw something special in this young man and recruited him to assist in further mission work. They became close companions. Paul sent Timothy on some of the more difficult assignments recorded in the New Testament. It is possible that Timothy was with Paul at this time in response to his request in 2 Timothy 4:9. This would mean the Prison Epistles were written after 2 Timothy, which is not a popular interpretation among scholars but fits well with the canonical evidence.[3]

Through this salutation, Paul has endeared himself to Philemon as someone who is suffering for the gospel. With the mention of Timothy, a well-known early Christian figure, Paul has also brought in a witness to this letter, holding Philemon to a degree of accountability.

2. Recipients (Philem. vv. 1b-2)

Next in the letter come the addressees, of whom there are three. The primary recipient is Philemon, the head of the household, who had the responsibility and authority for everything that happened in it. There is no record of when he became a believer, but possibly during Paul's extended ministry in the area. Paul, using terms of endearment, calls him a "dear friend and fellow worker" (v. 1*b*). Paul had obviously met Philemon at some point, and they had developed a close relationship upon which Paul could draw for his plea in this letter. Philemon had a church that met in his home (v. 2). A house church at that time might have around forty persons, about what an average Greco-Roman house might hold in its courtyard or open area. Perhaps it is Philemon's leadership of this church that moves Paul to call him a "fellow worker." Since Paul mentions this church, he probably intends the letter to be read out loud, creating accountability and putting positive social pressure on Philemon.

---

3. See Peter Walker, "Revisiting the Pastoral Epistles—Part I," *European Journal of Theology* 21, no. 1 (2012): 4-16; and Peter Walker, "Revisiting the Pastoral Epistles—Part II," *European Journal of Theology* 21, no. 2 (2012): 120-32.

Paul sends greetings to Apphia and Archippus (v. 2). Little is known of these people. Apphia has been interpreted since the early church as Philemon's wife, thus making them partners in the church that met in their home. Archippus is mentioned in Colossians 4:17 as having an important ministry that needed to be completed. Paul calls him here "our fellow soldier" (Philem. v. 2), which does not necessarily mean that he was a Roman soldier but that he was possibly involved in the mission of Christ (Phil. 2:25). This letter builds on the good relationship Paul had with Philemon.

3. Greetings (Philem. v. 3)

The next typical part of the opening of a letter is the greeting section. The letter to Philemon has Paul's signature greeting, "grace and peace," which is found in all of his letters. This is a combination of the Hellenistic *chairein* (greetings) and the Jewish *shalom* (peace). The Greek *chairein* shares the same root as Paul's *charis* ("grace"). Paul intends more than a social greeting. These words are filled with theological significance. The sources for these are "God our Father and the Lord Jesus Christ." These blessings are God's answer to the problem of sin. Grace is God's gift of salvation and mercy toward rebellious humanity, and peace is the result of reconciliation and forgiveness. The opening verses, as with all of Paul's letters, set the tone for the rest of the letter. Philemon can be assured that God is with him and that he is part of a great team that includes Paul and Timothy.

Thanksgiving (Philem. vv. 4-7)

Typical Hellenistic letters began with a thanksgiving to the gods that sets the tone for what follows. The technical word for this part of a letter is *exordium*, which focuses the attention of the readers and introduces key ideas. Paul follows this basic structure but "Christianizes" it and gives thanks to God for something God has done for the readers. This is the

shortest of any thanksgiving in Paul's letters, but nevertheless, it indicates
a lot about Paul's intention in the letter (as noted earlier, the thanksgiving
is missing in Galatians, 2 Corinthians, 1 Timothy, and Titus). This section can be divided into three parts: thanksgiving (vv. 4-5) and prayer (v.
6)—with the two being related, followed by a statement of how God has
answered Paul's prayer (v. 7).

Prayer was a habit of Paul's spiritual journey, as indicated by the adverb
"always" in verse 4. Often he gives thanks in his letters for the very issues
he will raise later. In verse 5, he gives two reasons for his thankfulness:
Philemon's love and faith, both of which are important themes in this
letter. Love and faith are often paired (along with hope) in Paul's letters
(1 Cor. 13:13; 2 Cor. 8:7; Gal. 5:6; Eph. 1:15; 6:23; Col. 1:4; 1 Thess.
3:6; 2 Thess. 1:3; 1 Tim. 1:5; 2:15; 6:11; 2 Tim. 1:13; Titus 2:2). Faith
is the topic of verse 6 of Philemon, and love is the topic of verse 7. The
structure of verse 5 is odd in the Greek because it is difficult to know how
to interpret the last phrase: "[which] you have toward the Lord Jesus and
for all the saints" (ESV). A simple reading takes the pair "love and faith" as
being for both Jesus and believers. It may simply mean that Philemon has
been loving and faithful to both; he has shown his love and faith to Jesus
as a testimony to the church that meets in his house. Paul is thankful that
Philemon has shown this type of spiritual maturity.

In verse 6, Paul's practice of prayer moves from thanksgiving to petition. God is answering Paul's prayer about Philemon's faith. The challenge
is how to interpret the phrase, "fellowship of . . . faith" (NASB). Fellowship requires sharing with someone or something, so with whom is Philemon's faith in partnership? The NIV adds "with us," but that is not part
of the text. There is no clear answer to this question, but two things are
clear: God was answering Paul's prayer, and Philemon's faith was growing
and deepening in the knowledge of the good that Christ was doing in the

lives of believers. Anything that Paul asks in this letter is built on the solid foundation of Philemon's growing faith!

Verse 7 indicates that Philemon's love has also grown. God's answer to Paul's prayer has returned to Paul in the form of "joy and encouragement." Word of Philemon's growth has "refreshed the hearts [*splanchna*; see v. 12 below] of the Lord's people [lit. "holy ones"]" and brought encouragement to others. Philemon is a model for what God through Christ can do in a person's life. Paul is thankful and excited to know that Philemon is carrying on the ministry in Colossae.

Body (Philem. vv. 8-20)

1. *Letter Theme (Philem. vv. 8-12)*

Verse 8 marks the beginning of the body of the letter (indicated by Gk. *dio* [therefore]), where Paul will begin to lay out the reason he is writing to Philemon. Rather than charging straight to his petition, he begins with his choice of motivation. He could come with the authority of an apostle of Jesus Christ (Paul is "bold enough" to do this if he had to [ESV]), but instead he has chosen the way of love. Verse 9 is the third mention of love in this short letter. This reveals a lot about Paul, that his life and vocabulary were filled with thoughts of love. Part of the support for the case he is building is his *ethos*. Ethos speaks to the believability and persuasiveness of the character of the speaker or writer. To his appeal from love Paul adds the mention of his old age and current imprisonment (see v. 1). He basically is pulling at Philemon's heartstrings. Paul must write carefully because he is going countercultural. He uses the indirect rhetorical method known as *insinuatio* to gain rapport with Philemon.[4] He must appeal to Philemon's Christian faith and not to his Hellenistic (legal) background. The way of love supersedes the route of the law (see 1 Cor. 6:1-8).

---

4. Ben Witherington III, *The Letters to Philemon, the Colossians, and the Ephesians: A Socio-Rhetorical Commentary on the Captivity Epistles* (Grand Rapids: Eerdmans, 2007), 61.

Verse 10 of Philemon finally gives the *propositio*, or focus, of Paul's request. Verses 10-12 make up one sentence in the Greek, causing Paul's appeal to be multifaceted and indirect. The key person of the letter is now introduced, although in the Greek his name is not given until the end of verse 10. Paul uses many descriptions of Onesimus in these verses that indicate the special relationship Paul had developed with him. First, Onesimus is Paul's spiritual "child," and Paul is his "father" (see 1 Cor. 4:15, 17). Evidently, Onesimus had come in contact with the imprisoned Paul, heard the gospel, and come to faith in Jesus Christ. Second, Onesimus has become useful for Paul in his current situation. Verse 11 of Philemon includes a wordplay on Onesimus's name, which means "profitable." Third, Onesimus is Paul's "heart" (v. 12). The word often translated as "heart" (*splanchna*) refers to the deep affection one feels at the gut level (see v. 7). Onesimus has worked his way into Paul's deepest affections and now has a special place in his life.

The relationship of Onesimus to Philemon has also now changed. Since Paul is Onesimus's spiritual father, this makes Philemon and Onesimus brothers in Christ (v. 16). Onesimus now is useful to Philemon as a coworker in the "fellowship of [the] faith" (v. 6, NASB), although Paul does not say specifically how. But as a Christian brother, Onesimus can now help in the ministry of the house church. Paul's plan is simple: he wants to send Onesimus back but expects a different type of situation for him when he arrives. Therein lies the problem: How will Philemon respond, with the law or with love?

2. Support for the Appeal (Philem. vv. 13-16)

Verses 13-16 serve as the *narratio*—that is, the background information that helps support the key request. Verse 13 builds on the idea of Onesimus's usefulness. Paul would like to have kept Onesimus with him but took the risk of sending him back with this letter, expecting Philemon's positive response. Why did he send Onesimus back and not just keep him as his helper? He may have felt that reconciliation needed to take place, both for Onesimus's sake as a new believer and for Philemon's sake as a step in his growing faith and love. It is unclear what type of help Philemon provided or could have provided to Paul in prison. Other churches sent Paul assistance (Phil. 2:25). Verse 14 of Philemon shows that Paul would not keep Onesimus with him without Philemon's consent. Paul honored Philemon's place as the master and did not want to coerce him in any way. A relationship of love must be voluntary.

In verse 15, Paul gives another reason for sending Onesimus back with this petition. This verse could be interpreted to mean that there was "perhaps" (*tacha*) a divine plan at work in Onesimus meeting Paul. The verb "was separated" (*echōristhē*) is passive, with God as the implied actor. Paul shifts Philemon's attention "from individual wrongs he may have incurred to God's providence which has made these wrongs work for good."[5] Before, the relationship between the master Philemon and the slave Onesimus was tenuous and temporary, but now the relationship between these new brothers was eternal as part of the family of God (v. 16). Verse 16 is the first mention that Onesimus was a slave. Paul calls him a "beloved [*agapēton*] brother" (NASB), which is the fourth time "love" is used in the letter. Whatever Onesimus's legal status may be, even if Philemon freed him, Philemon could no longer see him as the old slave he was before. They are brothers, on the same level before Christ. The key idea is found at the end of v. 16: Onesimus is "in the Lord" and now united with Christ, which should lead to a deeper fellowship with one another that transcends human divisions (see Gal. 3:28).

---

5. Peter T. O'Brien, *Introductory Thanksgivings in the Letters of Paul* (Leiden, NL: E. J. Brill, 1977), 295.

3. *Restatement and Final Appeal (Philem. vv. 17-20)*

Verses 17-22 summarize Paul's appeal to Philemon in what is known as the *peroratio*. Witherington points out the four elements in a good *peroratio*: restatement of the request (v. 17), amplification (vv. 18-19), emotional appeal (v. 20), and sealing of the bargain (vv. 21-22).[6] Verse 17 returns (marked by the transition "therefore" or "then" [*oun*]) to the theme of the letter and completes the content of the request in verse 10. The intent of this letter is now clear: Paul wants Philemon to welcome Onesimus back as if he were welcoming Paul himself. The request is built on the common bond (*koinōnon* ["partner" or "sharer"]) he has with Philemon. This bond is Christ. Paul has been careful with his wording in order to place the decision for reconciliation in the hands of Philemon. Even the request of verse 17 is stated as a conditional sentence. Paul's method in writing this letter is to provide the background, build the case, appeal especially to Philemon's faith, and then make the request. Not all letters follow this method. Paul can be forceful and authoritative when he needs to be (such as with the Galatians), but even then, he points to the power of love and the way of the cross (Gal. 2:20; 5:13, 14, 22; 6:14).

In verse 18 of Philemon, Paul wants to resolve any potential problems, and one of those might be that Onesimus owes Philemon money. This hints at possibly why Onesimus might be reluctant to return to Colossae. Paul adds assurance as a further support to his request that he personally will take care of any damage Onesimus has caused. Verse 19 continues the thought of verse 18 and serves as a form of IOU and promissory note that Paul would compensate Philemon. Paul tacks on an important idea: Philemon owes Paul an even more expensive debt—his very life! It may have been through Paul's ministry that Philemon was converted. Philemon had experienced the same grace of God through Christ as Onesimus, and so

---

6. Witherington, *Letters*, 83.

now they are on the same level. Rhetorically, this adds further pressure upon Philemon to follow Paul's directives.

In verse 20, Paul continues to build on the brotherly love he and Philemon share. He uses the style of rhetoric called *pathos*, which is an appeal to the emotions. The word "benefit" (*onaimēn*) is close to Onesimus's name. Paul again tugs at Philemon's heart by mentioning again the word *splanchna* (see vv. 7, 12). Philemon had refreshed the "hearts" of the saints by his love and faith, and now Paul wants him to extend his love and show his faith by welcoming Onesimus back as a brother in Christ. The result will be that Paul's own "deep inner person" will also be refreshed.

Closing (Philem. vv. 21-25)

With verse 21, Paul begins to move to the formal closing of the letter with one final appeal about the situation. The letter shows that Paul has seen Philemon's spiritual growth and is confident that Philemon will listen to his letter and respond in the appropriate way ("obedience" [NIV]; Gk., *hypakoē*, related to hearing [lit., "hearing below"]). Paul often includes at the end of his letters a "travelogue" (Rom. 15:14-33; 1 Cor. 4:14-21). Accordingly, as one final rhetorical move in verse 22 of Philemon, Paul mentions his travel plans and requests Philemon to prepare a guest room for him. Paul often expresses a desire to be with the people to whom he writes. He expected or at least hoped to be released from prison and have the opportunity to visit Colossae again. There is no record in the canon of the New Testament that he ever did this. This visit, if achievable, could serve as a follow-up to see how the situation was resolved.

Another element of the closing of a letter is the inclusion of personal greetings. Here, Paul mentions various people who were with him presumably in Rome when he wrote the letter (vv. 23-24). The assumption is that Philemon and the house church in Colossae knew these people (see above). Paul's other letters have similar greetings (Rom. 16 is the longest).

The last verse of the letter is in the form of a simple blessing (Philem. v. 25). All of Paul's letters have some form of closing benediction. It is in the form of a wish prayer, but the verb "be" must be supplied. This blessing is intended for the whole house church, as the plural "your" indicates. There are three significant descriptions of Jesus in this verse. He is the source of grace (see v. 3); the Lord—a significant claim for Paul to make, since he would soon appear before the lord Nero; and the Messiah—the fulfillment of God's plan of salvation.

A Call to Deeper Relationships

Once we begin to understand the details of this letter, we may find ourselves challenged to reevaluate how we interact with other people. The letter offers little as far as major theological ideas but reveals a lot about relationships. Although on the surface this appears to be a short personal letter of request, it is written by someone who built his life on his relationship with Jesus Christ. Paul believed this relationship with Christ transforms every other relationship a person may have. Each of the three primary characters in this letter provides a challenge to us about relationships.

Philemon was part of the second generation of Christians and had come in contact with Paul at some point and may have been converted through his ministry in the Lycus Valley. Philemon as a householder and slave owner was a man of power and position in that culture. He had the authority and right to demand Onesimus's return and to even have him punished. However, there is never any hint in this letter that Philemon is that type of person. Rather, what we find is someone with a deepening love and faith for Jesus and a desire to lead his house church deeper into this love and faith. When Paul thought of Philemon and prayed for him, happy thoughts of thanksgiving filled his heart and mind. Through love Philemon had developed a positive reputation and was making a difference in his house church. Here was evidence that the gospel changes people. Philemon still had to make a choice that would cause him to break the social norms around him. What would people think when he accepted his runaway slave back with open arms? Even more, what would happen if he viewed Onesimus as a partner and brother in the ministry! The gospel radically challenges our social practices and calls us to a higher level of love as new creations in Christ. Every human structure we have must be reevaluated in the light of love. This letter is an expression of deep Christian love, which is not bounded by human categories and divisions.

We also see the compassionate and personal side of Paul. This letter is full of Paul's affection and love for Philemon and Onesimus. Something radical had happened in Paul's life. This is not the Saul of Acts 9:1-2. Paul writes out of the overflow of his heart. He carefully negotiates a difficult situation through his endearing rhetoric of love. He lifts up Onesimus as a brother in the Lord and also preserves Philemon's authority as the leader of the household. He trusts that Philemon will do the right thing and accept Onesimus back as a Christian brother. This approach is risky, but obviously Paul had confidence in what God was doing in Philemon's life. The type of pressure he puts on Philemon to go in this direction is open, honest, and without hidden agenda. This type of approach should mark those whose hearts are filled with love. What is in our hearts will overflow onto our interactions with others. Paul uses many different terms for his friends in this letter that reveal his relationships, especially with Philemon: "partner," "brother," "beloved friend" (NKJV), "fellow laborer" (NKJV), "beloved" (NKJV), "fellow soldier," "my own heart" (NKJV), and "beloved brother" (NKJV). Love is

> This letter is an expression of deep Christian love, which is not bounded by human categories and divisions.

powerful and can bring people together from different backgrounds. Even while in prison, Paul was surrounded by people he loved and who loved him. He nurtured these relationships and served as a mentor to those who were with him, such as Timothy and Onesimus. Through this short letter, he also mentored Philemon, who was a thousand miles away.

Finally, the focus of this letter is on the outcome for Onesimus, the runaway slave who is now a new Christian brother in Christ. Onesimus had become a new person and would never be the same after this (2 Cor. 5:17). Would Philemon accept this change in Onesimus? Would he extend his love and faith to Onesimus? What effect did Paul's letter have upon this situation? The canon of the New Testament does not record anything further about what happened. Church tradition, however, offers some clues. One is that this letter was preserved and eventually canonized in the New Testament, which suggests it accomplished its purpose. Philemon did not tear up the letter and throw it away once he read it. Rather, he saw power in its words, kept it, and shared it with others. Another interesting possibility is the mention of the name Onesimus in Ignatius's letter *To the Ephesians*.[7] Ignatius (d. ca. AD 108/140) was the bishop of Syrian Antioch. Tradition states that he was martyred in Rome by being thrown to wild beasts possibly as early as 108 under the emperor Trajan (r. AD 98–117), but the date of this is uncertain. The date usually given for his letter to the Ephesians is about AD 110, which would be within the lifetime of a young Onesimus of Paul's day. By that time, Ephesus was one of the major centers of early Christianity. If this is the same Onesimus, then not only did Philemon free him, but also Onesimus went on to become one of the key leaders in the early church, which might also be why this letter was preserved and included in the Pauline corpus. We never know how far the ripple effect of one changed life may go.

---

7. Ignatius, *To the Ephesians* 1:3; 2:1; 6:2, in *The Apostolic Fathers*, 86, 87, 88.

Every society has inequalities. Those people at the lower end of a society often end up oppressed and victimized. Slavery in the first century was a form of human trafficking where people were considered property to be used and sometimes abused for the pleasures and purposes of an owner. The gospel challenged this situation and promoted a new bond of unity where masters and slaves became brothers and sisters. Human trafficking destroys individuals and families and leaves a hole in the heart of a society. It ruins the safety and security of innocent people who end up living in fear of being exploited. This letter challenges us not to become blind to the atrocities around us. We must remove whatever is blinding people to social injustices and remove the barriers that divide people. Like Paul, we find the resources for all of this in our love for and faith in Jesus Christ. The world has a difficult time understanding the type of love displayed in this letter. When the Spirit of Christ comes and lives in us, we begin to take on the characteristics of Christ, particularly an unconditional love for others. New relationships are developed when we are united under the lordship of Jesus Christ. The bonds of kinship within the church should bring forgiveness, reconciliation, renewal, and purpose. As Philemon experienced, the church is where this love is best learned and lived out. This letter shows how the world can be changed through love and faith.

This is a letter about surrender and acts of faith. Paul was calling Philemon to surrender his possession of Onesimus. Paul had to release Onesimus back to Philemon. Onesimus had to risk trusting in God's purposes for him even though he did not know the outcome.

4

Prayers, Doxologies, and Benedictions

EPHESIANS 3:14-21

Prayer in Paul's Ministry

Paul's letters contain different liturgical forms. These forms are often recognizable because of their special vocabulary or grammatical structure. This unique literature takes on its recognizable form over time due to repeated use in public worship, such as with "psalms, hymns, and songs from the Spirit" (Eph. 5:19). Interpreters do not always agree that a particular passage in Paul's letters is necessarily liturgical or that Paul had adopted or adapted it from a form that had a wider usage. Some liturgical passages are relatively easy to recognize because they stand out from their literary context. Modern translations often indicate this assumption by indenting the passage. The early church developed simple creeds that briefly stated its faith and were recited in public worship. These often are introduced with an introductory formula indicating acceptance in the church, especially of a belief related to the saving work of Christ (1 Cor. 15:3-5; 1 Tim. 3:16). Hymns may have been used as part of corporate worship (Eph. 5:19-20; Col. 3:16). They are similar to creeds but are introduced with the relative pronoun "who" (Eph. 2:14-16; Phil. 2:6-11; Col. 1:15-20). It is unclear if Paul wrote these hymns or if he is quoting or paraphrasing hymns of the early church.

One significant liturgical form seen throughout Paul's letters is prayer. Prayer was a vital part of his life. His entire ministry was saturated with prayer. He inherited his lifestyle of prayer from his Jewish roots. The Old Testament records many prayers in the Psalms and Prophets. Rabbis used both formal and spontaneous prayers throughout the day. Prayer was viewed as an essential requirement for those seeking to be righteous. Directly after his Damascus road vision, Paul spent three days in prayer and fasting (Acts 9:9, 11). He did not write direct prayers to God in his letters by specifically addressing God in the second person singular ("God, may you . . ."), but indirect wish prayers using the third person, often using the rare optative mood in Greek: "May God . . ." (Rom. 15:5, 13; 1 Thess. 3:11-13; 5:23). As Acts records, prayer was a sustaining power of Paul's evangelistic ministry throughout the Roman Empire. He began his first journey as a result of the prayer and fasting of the Antioch church (Acts 13:2-3). At times, his prayers included singing, as in the Philippian jail (16:25). Miracles often accompanied his prayers (28:8).

Paul's letters show constant vigil in prayer (1 Thess. 5:17). Many of his letters begin with a specific reference to how he "always" prayed for the churches (Phil. 1:4; Col. 1:3; 1 Thess. 1:2; 2 Thess. 1:3; Philem. v. 4). He uses sixteen different words for prayer 105 different times. He encouraged the churches to pray for him (Rom. 15:30) about specific matters of ministry (2 Thess. 3:1-2). He believed that prayer made a difference in the effectiveness of his ministry (Col. 4:3-4). The prayers of others helped him know what to say when he preached (Eph. 6:19-20).

The letters display several types of prayer. Doxologies are short statements of praise to God, often occurring at the end of a prayer. They come as a result of something significant Paul wrote that spurred him to express praise for some attribute of God. They are easy to recognize because they have a fairly common threefold structure. At the beginning is a mention of God, next is a word of praise acknowledging God's glory or some other attribute, and then comes a concluding temporal description, often ending with "amen." There are many examples of doxologies in Paul's letters, some short (1 Tim. 6:16; 2 Tim. 4:18) and some much longer (Rom. 11:33-36; 2 Cor. 1:3-11). Benedictions are wish prayers often at the beginning (Rom. 1:7; Eph. 1:3-4) or ending of a letter. All of Paul's letters close with some type of benediction (1 Cor. 16:23; 2 Cor. 13:14; Gal. 6:18). He often expresses his prayers in the way of thanksgiving at the beginning of his letters (Rom. 1:8-15; 1 Thess. 1:2-10). His thanksgivings and petitions show his "deep pastoral . . . concern for the addressees."[1] They often reveal problems that Paul will discuss later in the letter (1 Cor. 1:4-9).

Prayer was a way for Paul to express his response to what God had done, was doing, and would do in Jesus Christ. His motivation for prayer may have been his utter dependency upon God's grace. Paul knew the ravages of sin and the hopelessness of self-righteousness. His testimony in 1 Timothy 1:12-17 is enveloped with thanksgiving in verse 12*a* and a doxology in verse 17. Prayer connects us with God through the presence of the Holy Spirit, who intercedes in our prayers (Rom. 8:26-27; Eph. 6:18). Prayer is experiencing God's presence in a deep personal fellowship that influences all of one's life.

Many of Paul's prayers show careful wording, which invites a close reading of them. Even with limited knowledge of Greek, modern interpreters can discover useful insights by asking questions and looking for answers from the author. One method that has proven beneficial is called "phrasing." This type of interpretation breaks a passage apart into small units (phrases or clauses) and studies how these relate to one another, or the *syntax*. The goal is to determine the flow of thought of the author and

---

1. O'Brien, *Introductory Thanksgivings*, 262.

the key points he or she is making. Phrasing is supported by defining key words and grammatical structures. Knowing Greek is a benefit because it shows the relationship of words through the use of the various case endings. If the interpreter does not know Greek, however, the next best option is to use a literal English translation, such as the ESV or NASB. Some knowledge of English grammar can also be helpful. The steps are as follows:

1. Identify the beginning and ending of a passage (such as a paragraph).

2. Break the passage down into phrases or clauses (dependent, independent, adverbial, adjectival, prepositional, etc.). For many modern English translations, start with the obvious punctuation: commas, semicolons, colons, hyphens, and so on. With practice, you can be more grammatically precise. One simple method is to note natural breaks—that is, when a person might pause and take a breath or a break in the sentence as if he or she were doing a "responsive reading" in church.

3. Identify and copy the main clause(s) to the far left of a sheet of paper. This will include the subject, finite verb, and indirect and direct objects.

4. Identify any subordinate clauses or phrases that modify other clauses and phrases and are dependent on them for their meanings. The most useful way to do this is to ask questions using the words of one phrase to answer the question from another phrase. On your sheet of paper, put the modifying phrases directly under or over the phrases they modify. For semantic relationships that are equal, parallel, or in a series, align them together.

5. For more advanced study, one can note the semantic relationship between the clauses.

This method can be used with helpful results in most of Paul's letters because of the careful wording and sequence of his rhetorical arguments. Ephesians 3:14-21 is a prayer that is particularly difficult to interpret because of its complex structure. Verses 14-19 are one complex sentence in the original Greek. Most English translations break it down into smaller sentences because of its complexity. The result is that some of the details of this prayer are missed. Doing a careful phrasing of this passage will reveal the key points of Paul's prayer.

Traditionally, the author of Ephesians has been accepted as Paul, but modern scholars have raised doubts about this because of its style, similarity to Colossians, and advanced theology. The issues related to this discussion are complex. In my opinion, there are strong reasons to accept this letter as authentic, particularly because of the Pauline themes that are present throughout the letter. Evidently, Paul was in prison when he wrote the letter (3:1; 4:1), although it is not clear which imprisonment. If this was his Roman imprisonment, the date would be the early AD 60s. One challenge about the letter is that the reference "in Ephesus" in 1:1 is not found in the earliest known manuscripts. This suggests that the original letter may have been intended as a circular letter—that is, a letter to be passed around among many churches.

Paul had a fruitful ministry in Ephesus. He had a short visit there after leaving Corinth (Acts 18:18-22) and returned later for two years (ch. 19), making this one of the longest stays of his ministry. Later, the Ephesian church had been infiltrated by false teachers, so Paul sent Timothy there and later wrote his two letters to help Timothy guide the Ephesian church during that time. It is difficult to determine why Paul wrote this letter. The prayer of Ephesians 3:14-21 comes at the end of the doctrinal section and serves as a transition to the exhortation of 4:1–6:9. If the position of this prayer can be any clue, Paul wanted the Ephesians to be unified in purpose, grounded in the love of God, and in pursuit of all that God had planned for them in Christ.

A Prayer for Deepening Love

Phrasing this passage produces six sections, as determined by the grammatical structures in the Greek. I will use my own literal translation so that the original grammatical structures can be preserved as much as possible. The non-Greek student might use the ESV to arrive at similar results. The six major parts are as follows: The main clause is found in verse 14, followed by four dependent and interlinked clauses in verses 16-19. Three of these begin with the Greek word *hina*, which is used to show purpose or result. Verses 20-21 become their own unit in the form of a doxology. The structure, syntax, grammar, and key words of each of these six parts will be analyzed in order to determine the primary goals of Paul's prayer. Words that are underlined in the following diagrams are what the following clauses or phrases in each section are syntactically dependent upon.

MAIN CLAUSE
(Eph. 3:14-15)

For this reason [the logical transition from the earlier section
that links this passage with what comes before]

I bow my knees [the main clause of vv. 14-19]

before the Father [where I bow my knees],

from whom every family in heaven and on

earth is named ["who" is the Father], . . .
(Vv. 14-15, AT)

Fig. 4.1. Main clause

The opening transition links this passage to the previous passage, urging us to consider the literary context (see fig. 4.1). Verse 1 begins with exactly the same type of transition, linking this chapter back especially to 2:11-22. It becomes evident that Paul is systematically building an argument that ends with this prayer. Ephesians 4:1 begins the paraenesis (exhortation) section of the letter, since Paul expects certain responses to God's gracious work described in Ephesians 1–3. Paul has just described his gospel as the "mystery of Christ" that calls all people to partake in God's promises in Christ (3:1-6). Paul has become personally involved in preaching this gospel because of God's revelation to him. Verses 14-21 constitute Paul's prayer for how the Ephesians can fully participate in this glorious gospel.

The main verb of the sentence informs us that this is a prayer. Kneeling in prayer was a sign of deep reverence for God.[2] The more typical Jewish way to pray was standing, as Jesus mentioned in Mark 11:25. Kneeling is a way to show humility, dependence, and worship. Early Christians often knelt in prayer (Acts 7:60; 9:40; 20:36; 21:5). Paul is physically involved in this prayer of intercession.

Paul can pray with assurance because of the one to whom he is praying. The Father is the awesome creator of all families. The term *patria* (family) is related to the same word as "father" (*patera*) and shows origin and orientation (Eph. 3:14-15).[3] The idea of one Father of all families speaks to the unity about which Paul has been writing. Both Jews and Gentiles have become one body in Christ (2:16) because the "dividing wall of hostility" has been removed (v. 14). The result is that "there is one body and one Spirit . . . one hope . . . one Lord, one faith, one baptism; one God and Father of all" (4:4-6). This statement also has the effect of highlighting God's greatness over all that has been created. He is sovereign and able to answer this prayer.

---

2. Lincoln, *Ephesians*, 202.

3. G. Schrenk, *patēr*, in *Theological Dictionary of the New Testament*, ed. Gerhard Kittel and Gerhard Friedrich, trans. Geoffrey W. Bromiley (Grand Rapids: Eerdmans, 1967), 5:1017.

PURPOSE CLAUSE ONE

(Eph. 3:16)

I bow my knees . . . [v. 14]

in order that he may grant you to be strengthened [the purpose of Paul's prayer]

according to the riches of his glory [how you will be strengthened]

with power [how you will be strengthened]

through his Spirit [the source of the power and strength]

in your inner person [where you will be strengthened], . . . (Vv. 14, 16, AT)

Fig. 4.2. Purpose clause one

Paul shows the reason for his prayer by using a purpose clause indicated in the Greek with *hina* followed by a verb in the subjunctive mood (see fig. 4.2). A purpose clause is indicated in English with the words "that" or "in order that." The passive infinitive "to be strengthened" completes the idea of the verb. This grammatical construction indicates that the first goal of Paul's prayer is that the Father would strengthen the Ephesians.

There are three phrases that describe this strengthening. The first is the resource for this strengthening: the very riches of God's glory. God's glory is an important theme in Paul's letters and all of Scripture. God's glory is representative of his radiant holiness and awesome power that compels humanity to fall down in worship. Our goal as creatures is to be found worthy to be in a relationship with the Holy God by taking on more of his divine nature (2 Cor. 3:18; Col. 3:4). Sin separates us from God's glory but can be remedied because of God's grace in Jesus Christ that is accepted in humble faith (Rom. 3:23-24). Paul is not asking for a small bit of God's glory but the abundant "riches" (*ploutos*; Eph. 1:7, 18; 2:7; 3:8). God's glory is overwhelming, but Paul is asking for "grace upon grace" (John 1:16, NASB). Second, the source of strength is "power" (Eph. 3:16). The Holy Spirit is the source of this power that comes from the Father and is resourced through his glory. Third, this strengthening will take place in one's inner "person" (v. 16, AT; see 2 Cor. 4:16). "Person" here comes from the Greek word often translated as "human." In other places, Paul describes the inner place of our lives as the "mind," the place where we make decisions that influence how we live and think (Rom. 8:5; 12:2; 1 Cor. 2:16; Phil. 2:5; Col. 3:2). If our essential, inner person is strengthened with the power of the Holy Spirit so that we experience God's glory and take on more of his holy character, then our worldview will be significantly altered and how we live will be conformed more to God's holy and loving purposes for us.

PURPOSE CLAUSE TWO
(Eph. 3:17*a*)

be strengthened . . . [v. 16]

so that Christ *may dwell* [the result of God's strengthening]

through faith [how Christ will dwell]

in your hearts [where Christ will dwell], . . .
(Vv. 16-17*a*, AT)

Fig. 4.3. Purpose clause two

The first purpose clause leads Paul to consider the outcome of God's strengthening. This outcome can be expressed as the goal, result, or purpose of the strengthening. This is indicated in the above diagram (fig. 4.3) by placing this clause directly under the idea it modifies: "be strengthened." Paul uses a different type of grammatical construction with an infinitive followed by its subject in the accusative case to show purpose,[4] making this a second purpose clause in this prayer. This second purpose construction is closely linked grammatically to the first purpose clause. What will God's strengthening do for us? The aorist tense of the infinitive suggests that God's strengthening will enable Christ to "take up residence." His home will be "in your hearts." "Hearts" here is similar in meaning to the "inner person" of the earlier phrase in verse 16. This is where the Spirit transforms us and guides us into holy living. The way to experience Christ deep within our person is "through faith" (Eph. 3:17*a*). This does not happen accidently but only through committing ourselves to the supremacy of Christ. An act of total consecration is required for the goal of this prayer to become a reality. As Paul wrote in Galatians 2:20, Christ's living in us comes through crucifying the old life. The goal of this prayer is for the

4. Daniel B. Wallace, *Greek Grammar beyond the Basics* (Grand Rapids: Zondervan, 1996), 590-92.

PURPOSE CLAUSE THREE

(Eph. 3:17b-19a)

may dwell . . . [v. 17]

by being rooted and grounded in love [how we have strength],

so that you may be strengthened to understand [the result of Christ's dwelling in us]

    with all the saints [those who know this love]

    what is the breadth and [series describing this love]

        length and

        height and

        depth,

    and to know the <u>love</u> of Christ [result of the strengthening]

        that surpasses knowledge [describes this love], . . .
        (Vv. 17-19a, AT)

Fig. 4.4. Purpose clause three

Ephesians to be completely sanctified by putting off the old person and being recreated in the loving likeness of God seen in Christ Jesus (Eph. 4:22-24; 5:1-2). Paul is praying that they will experience God's plan for them in Christ by totally trusting in Christ as Lord of their thoughts and intentions. This is the very reason we have been created (1:3-4).

The third purpose clause is tightly structured and requires careful analysis (see fig. 4.4). The whole clause reflects back on Christ's indwelling from verse 17. When Christ dwells in our hearts, the result will be strength. In verse 18, the aorist subjunctive verb *exischysēte* (you may be strengthened [AT]) more precisely means "to be fully capable of doing or experiencing something."[5] The only way we can experience the love of Christ is for Christ to dwell in our hearts. Any knowledge that is not grounded in this type of relationship is inadequate and partial.

It is difficult in English to know what to do with the phrase "being rooted and grounded in love" at the end of verse 17. This awkward phrase is made of two perfect passive participles. Greek participles are often related to another word in form and meaning. This can be determined by looking at the case ending. Both of these participles are in the nominative case. Because they have no article, they are likely adverbial participles modifying the verb *exischysēte*. Adverbial participles always beg for the interpretation of what type of action they are describing. The easiest way to determine this is to ask questions. In this case, these participles answer *how* we may be strengthened: "*by* being rooted and grounded." The passive voice indicates that this is something done to us. The context of verse 16 suggests that this is done through the power of the indwelling Holy Spirit. The perfect tense of these participles suggests that we begin to be built up in love when the Holy Spirit sanctifies us as a result of our faith in Christ. The meaning of these participles offers the image of a plant

---

5. Bauer et al., *Greek-English Lexicon*, 350.

root digging deeply into the earth so that it is healthy, vigorous, and well supported. "Love is the soil in which believers are to be rooted and grow, the foundation on which they are to be built."[6] The source of this love is not specified in this phrase, whether it is our love for Christ or his love for us. God is the source of all love, so it is not necessary to choose one or the other (see 2 Cor. 5:14; 1 John 4:7).

Paul is praying that the Ephesians will be strengthened to do two things, specified with two aorist infinitives with similar ideas: "to understand" (*katalabesthai*) and "to know" (*gnōnai*) (Eph. 3:18-19). The first word means "to process information, understand, grasp,"[7] an intensive learning to the point of having some mastery of the topic. The second word is the more common word for gaining knowledge, awareness, and learning. This grasping of love is done in community: "with all the saints." Knowing the love of God in Christ is the goal of all of God's people. Deep within the inner person, in the heart, there exists a special place reserved only for the sovereign Creator. The "holy ones" (saints), those who have been sanctified by the blood of Christ, are on the path of discovery and are grasping deep within themselves this love that "has been poured out into our hearts through the Holy Spirit, who has been given to us" (Rom. 5:5).

Paul describes the specific object of this experiential learning in another awkward phrase with four parallel predicate adjectives that simply modify the generic "what" (*ti*). The reader is compelled to look at the context to see what this is referencing. The sequence of thought in the next clause and the parallel structure of the two infinitives "to understand" and "to know" suggest that Paul is attempting to describe in poetic and lofty language the "love of Christ" in all its rich dimensions (see v. 19). This phrase reflects the same thought present in Romans 8:37-39. The love of Christ

---

6. Lincoln, *Ephesians*, 207.
7. Bauer et al., *Greek-English Lexicon*, 520.

is incomprehensible, even though we can come to know it partly in this life (1 Cor. 13:12).

The second infinitive, "to know," advances this idea (Eph. 3:19) and shows the tension between the "now and not yet" experience believers can have of the love of Christ. Christ's dwelling within us results in our knowing Christ's love more. It is a reciprocal relationship. We open our lives more to Christ's love, and he gives us more of this love. We press on to know the love of Christ, but we can never exhaust that love. There is always more to learn because it "surpasses knowledge" (v. 19).

PURPOSE CLAUSE FOUR
(Eph. 3:19*b*)

be strengthened . . . [v. 18]

    in order that you may be filled [the goal of being strengthened]

        with all the fullness of God
        [what we are filled with]. [Vv. 18, 19*b*, AT]

Fig. 4.5. Purpose clause four

Paul now reaches the climax of his intercessory prayer for the Ephesian church. The purpose of being strengthened in verse 18 is so that the Ephesian believers may experience the "fullness of God." This last purpose clause is linked to the previous clause as the last goal of Paul's prayer (see fig 4.5). The word "fill" (*plērō-*) is used twice in this verse. The verb "may be filled" (*plērōthēte*) is in the passive voice. When something awesome like this happens and a passive verb is used, it is often called a "divine passive." The assumption is that God does this filling in us. Verse 16 indicates that this filling is through the indwelling Spirit. This filling has a specific goal, indicated in the Greek with the preposition *eis* followed by a word in the accusative case, "with the goal of fullness" (v. 19*b*, AT). "Fullness" (*plērōma*) denotes completeness.[8] This is God's plan and purpose for humanity. Paul will repeat and extend this idea in Ephesians 4:13 to show that the purpose of the church is to "reach unity in the faith and in the knowledge of the Son of God and become mature, attaining to the whole measure of the fullness of Christ." The Holy Spirit is the one who fills us with this fullness and transforms how we live (5:18). A parallel thought is found in Colossians 2:9-10: "For in Christ all the fullness of the Deity lives in bodily form, and in Christ you have been brought to fullness." The culmination of the believer's existence is to experience the fullness of the indwelling Christ through the sanctifying work of the indwelling Spirit.

The sequence of this prayer shows how this filling takes place. The main clauses of these verses can be graphed as follows, with the dependent phrases fitting in appropriate places as the above diagrams are combined (fig. 4.6). The underlined words are what each following phrase modifies:

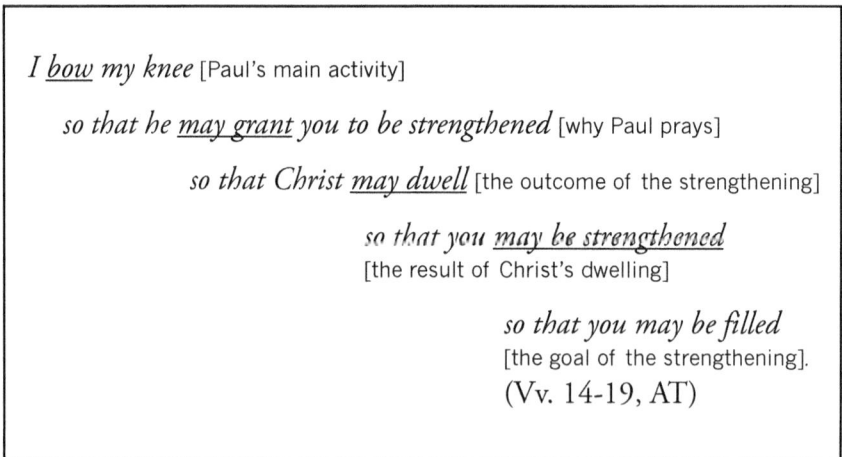

I bow my knee [Paul's main activity]

 so that he may grant you to be strengthened [why Paul prays]

  so that Christ may dwell [the outcome of the strengthening]

   so that you may be strengthened
   [the result of Christ's dwelling]

    so that you may be filled
    [the goal of the strengthening].
    (Vv. 14-19, AT)

Fig. 4.6. Sequence of clauses and phrases

In summary, Paul prays to the Father so that the Ephesians will be strengthened through the Holy Spirit so that Christ can dwell in them.

---

8. Ibid., 829.

When Christ is within a believer through the Holy Spirit, the result will be the ability to know the love of Christ in our innermost person, as God created us to experience. There are other ways to interpret the relationship of these phrases, but the above sequence flows naturally and shows a logical connection that can be supported from other parts of this letter and broader Pauline theology.

DOXOLOGY
(Eph. 3:20-21)

Now to the one who is <u>able to do</u> . . .

> *beyond all things*
>
> *more abundantly*
>
> > *. . . the things which we ask and think*
>
> *according to the <u>power</u>*
>
> > > *which is working in us.*
> > > (V. 20, AT)

Fig. 4.7. Doxology

Paul ends his prayer with a doxology, which is literally a "word of praise" (see fig. 4.7). Verses 20-21 make up one sentence in the Greek. It begins the way Romans 16:25 does: "now to him who is able." "Now" (*de*) links these verses to the previous prayer and shows that God is able to do everything Paul has asked in Ephesians 3:14-19. The object of praise in a doxology is usually in the dative case. "To the one" obviously refers to the Father of verse 14. This doxology focuses upon the qualities of God that assure the above prayer asking for the fullness of Christ through the Holy Spirit is possible. The reason God can answer this prayer is because he "is able." The word *dynamenō* (is able) denotes the power to accomplish.

Ephesians 1:19-20 states that God's "incomparably great power" is available "for us who believe. That power is the same as the mighty strength he exerted when he raised Christ from the dead and seated him at his right hand in the heavenly realms." This is the power that sanctifies us so that we may experience the fullness of the indwelling Christ (3:16). This same resurrection power can transform our enslaved inner person into a new creation (2 Cor. 5:17). The power at work within us is the Holy Spirit, who gives us the strength for this transformation into Christ's likeness.

God is able to do "beyond all things" (Eph. 3:20, AT), a generic but extravagant catchall that likely refers back to the prayer of Ephesians 3:14-19. "More abundantly" (AT) is a rare double compound adverb with two prefixes ("above" and "out of") and has the sense of superabundance (see 1 Thess. 3:10; 5:13).[9] What God can do is beyond our best imagination. Paul shifts to the first-person plural "we" to make this exhaustive statement also inclusive (Eph. 3:20). God is able to do this transformation because he has the power. This "power" is constantly "working in us" (AT; a present-tense participle from the word *energeō*—a root for the word "energy") to accomplish God's purposes for us in Christ (v. 20). This ascription of power shows that God can do incredible things, specifically, to restore us to his purposes and image (1:3-14; 4:24). This is a fitting end to the doctrinal/descriptive part of the letter.

> *To him <u>be glory</u>*
>> *in the church and*
>> *in Christ Jesus*
>> *into all generations*
>> *forever and ever. Amen.* (V. 21, AT)

Fig. 4.8. Ascription of glory

---

9. Witherington, *Letters*, 277.

Verse 21 extends the doxology further by ascribing glory to "the one who is able" (see fig. 4.8). The reason for this ascription of glory is given in verse 20. The verb "be" must be added, making this a declaration. Glory can only be given to God because only he deserves it. The opening statement is modified by three prepositional phrases and concludes with the typical time indicator. God's glory can be found in the three entities. This is the only doxology in the New Testament that includes a reference to the church and the phrase "in Christ Jesus." The church "is the sphere in which God's glory is acknowledged."[10]

Glory in the church is connected to being in Christ Jesus. To be "in Christ" is the profound and intimate relationship with Christ that results when we acknowledge him as Lord and Savior. Being in Christ makes us new creations (2 Cor. 5:17). We experience freedom from the control of sin (Rom. 6:4; 8:1-2) and power to live the sanctified life of unconditional love (Eph. 4:24; 5:1-2). Giving glory to God is the natural response of one who is in Christ. This word of praise and the promises and experiences that support it are unending and stretch across generations because this is the very nature of the triune God. The response of "amen" confirms the truth of this blessing.

This Prayer in Our Lives

Paul's prayer for the Ephesians continues to echo across the centuries with timeless truths that apply to any sincere seeker of the deeper life with God. This is not a selfish prayer asking for things on a wish list. It is not a prayer for health, wealth, and prosperity. It is not even a prayer that asks for God's blessings, even though verse 20 is often quoted in that regard. The essential truth is that God wants to do more in our lives to conform us to his purposes for us in Christ than we can ever think or imagine.

---

10. Lincoln, *Ephesians*, 217.

The four highlighted purpose clauses help us to focus on the heart of this prayer. Careful study of the English text may help the interpreter arrive at similar conclusions to the above, but much will be lost without a close reading of a literal translation and a study of the relationship of the phrases. This prayer opens the gate to the endless richness of new life in Jesus Christ. The Ephesian believers had started this journey, but Paul asks God to draw them further into his grace so that they may know more and more about how much God loves them.

The Christian life is not a matter of human intellect or ability but of God's power and grace experienced by the humble in heart. What keeps people from experiencing a prayer like this? They remain stuck in the old life Paul describes in Ephesians 4:17-19. They have hardened their hearts so that they do not hear what the Holy Spirit wants to do in them. They have given in to the pull of the flesh and its desires that feed selfishness and pride. The only way to experience this type of prayer is through the fully consecrated life. The life that has submitted to the lordship of Christ is open to the work of the Holy Spirit, which always leads us to transformation into Christ's image (4:24; 5:1-2). This deep experience of love is the essence of the life that has been entirely sanctified. This is not something we have to wait until we get to heaven to experience but is a promise for the present (1 Thess. 5:23-24).

This is a prayer not just for the individual but for the whole church (Eph. 3:18). We grow into Christ's likeness together. However, a person cannot hide in the group. Each person must make the decision of faith and commitment. This decision is then supported through the ministry of leaders who help each individual become bonded to others in the unity of faith and deep knowledge of the Son of God, with the ultimate goal of becoming mature and experiencing the fullness of God's plan for us in Christ (4:12-13). Because God's love is not easy to understand, we need our relationships with one another. It is in those relationships that we come to know the depth of the love of Christ. Isolation only feeds pride and selfishness. We need to "work out" this profound salvation together, "with fear and trembling," by taking on the self-giving mindset of Jesus (Phil. 2:5, 12-13). We may never be able to fully grasp this love, but we must seek it with all of our being. Our primary goal in this life is to know the love of God in Christ Jesus. We experience more as we yield more. We must never underestimate what God can do in our lives through this love.

5

Paul's Hermeneutical Method

ROMANS 9–11

Paul and Scripture

Paul had a profound reverence for Scripture and believed it to be the inspired oracles of God (Rom. 3:2) and useful in the church (2 Tim. 3:16-17). He insisted his message about Jesus was the fulfillment of God's promises in Scripture (Rom. 1:2; 16:25-26). He claimed "immediate revelatory illumination," whereas the rabbis appealed "to majority opinion within an interpretive community."[1] He quotes Scripture numerous times throughout his letters, ranging from eighty-five to one hundred times, depending on what is considered a quotation. He has at least twice as many allusions to Old Testament passages, stories, or characters. He used primarily the Septuagint (Greek translation of the Old Testament). Some quotations appear to use the Hebrew text, and others do not match either the Hebrew or Greek but seem to be more from memory or a paraphrase. At times, he does not cite a specific text, but it is clear that Old Testament themes stand behind his thinking. Since Scripture was so important to him, it is worthwhile to consider his methods in attempting to understand his thinking.

Paul's letters indicate that his Jewish past continued to influence his thinking. When he was arrested at the temple in Jerusalem, he told the gathered crowd, "I am a Jew, born in Tarsus of Cilicia, but brought up in this city. I studied under Gamaliel and was thoroughly trained in the law

---

1. Richard B. Hays, *Echoes of Scripture in the Letters of Paul* (New Haven, CT: Yale University Press, 1989), 4.

of our ancestors" (Acts 22:3). Gamaliel was one of the leading scholars of the time and was either a son or grandson of the renowned rabbi Hillel. Hillel developed a set of seven rules for interpreting Scripture. These rules became widely known and are preserved in the Mishnah.[2] They were expanded by other Jewish teachers after the New Testament period.

Paul later testified before the Sanhedrin, "I am a Pharisee, descended from Pharisees" (23:6). This is echoed in Philippians 3:5: "circumcised on the eighth day, of the people of Israel, of the tribe of Benjamin, a Hebrew of Hebrews; in regard to the law, a Pharisee." Pharisees were known for their zeal in keeping God's laws, including the oral interpretation of the Old Testament laws.

In Galatians 1:14, Paul writes that he was "extremely zealous for the traditions of [his] fathers." These "traditions" were a key topic of study for young Jewish scholars. Paul knew Hebrew (the language of the Old Testament), Aramaic (the dialect of Palestine), and Greek (the international language in which he wrote his letters). Jewish boys learned how to read the Hebrew Old Testament. Their education included learning interpretive methods, such as Hillel's seven rules, that helped them apply Scripture to their contemporary situations.

Rabbinic Judaism was primarily the legacy of the Pharisees at the end of the Second Temple period, which began with the rebuilding of the temple in 520-515 BC and ended with the temple's destruction in AD 70. Some of the interpretive methods used by the rabbis may be reflected in Paul's letters, although he was not bound solely to these methods. Many of the early rabbinic methods known today are found in literature written after Paul's lifetime, and so some caution is needed to avoid anachronisms.

Some of the common methods of Scripture interpretation included the following: *Peshat* is a literal interpretation of a passage that appeals to its

---

2. The principal and original part of the Oral Torah (Law), the Mishnah is a written compilation of Jewish oral legal traditions.

plain sense, such as Romans 3:4 citing Psalm 51:4. *Pesher* is the interpretation of a passage from the perspective of eschatological fulfillment. The Qumran community of Essenes used this method in the Dead Sea Scrolls. A possible example can be found in 2 Corinthians 6:2 and also in Paul's speech found in Acts 13:16-41. Allegory seeks a deeper spiritual meaning hidden behind the literal meaning of a text. Paul used an allegorical interpretation of Hagar and Sarah in Galatians 4:21-31. Typology is discerning a correspondence between people or events of the past and people or events of the present or future, with the conviction that how God acted in the past is how God acts later. In Romans 5:12-21 and 1 Corinthians 15:20-22, 45, the first Adam is compared as a type for Christ, who came as the "second Adam." *Midrash* is a form of Jewish commentary where an earlier interpretation, especially from a significant rabbi, is appealed to as authoritative. Paul does not cite any rabbi for authority or comment but does refer to early Christian tradition in 1 Corinthians 15:1-7. In other places, Paul uses a form of *midrash* to make comments on specific passages from the Old Testament.

Paul could not escape his Jewish past but reinterpreted it through his experience of the resurrected Jesus Christ. Perhaps most significant in his use of Scripture is his Christological interpretation of Jesus as "the revelation of the mystery hidden for long ages past, but now revealed and made known through the prophetic writings by the command of the eternal God" (Rom. 16:25-26; see 1 Cor. 15:3-4; Col. 1:26-27). His vision of the risen Jesus and direct commission to preach the gospel became the central paradigm for all he did, including his interpretation of Scripture (Gal. 1:11-12). Scripture was important to him but secondary to the full revelation of God's grace in Jesus.

The Epistle to the Romans contains more quotations from the Old Testament than any other Pauline Epistle, with a concentration of these in Romans 9–11. In these three chapters alone, Paul quotes or has clear allusions to at least thirty-three different Old Testament passages. These chapters pose many challenges to interpreters and unfortunately are often skipped over in personal study, teaching, and preaching. At best, these chapters are only given a cursory glance or are used to support a certain theological argument, such as predestination.

These chapters, however, are not a digression in the letter but build on Paul's basic thesis found in 1:16-17: "For I am not ashamed of the gospel, because it is the power of God that brings salvation to everyone who believes: first to the Jew, then to the Gentile. For in the gospel the righteousness of God is revealed—a righteousness that is by faith from first to last, just as it is written: 'The righteous will live by faith.'" These verses make several assertions that guide Paul's thoughts throughout the letter. First, the gospel contains the power of God, the same power that created the universe and raised Jesus from the dead. Second, the gospel brings salvation through Jesus Christ and is available to everyone. Third, Jews and Gentiles (which basically covers all people) must obtain this salvation the same way: through God's grace accepted by believing in Jesus Christ. Fourth, believers are made righteous through freedom from sin's condemnation and power, bringing growth in grace leading to Christlikeness.

In Romans 3:21–8:39, Paul demonstrates that both Jews and Gentiles can participate in this good news. Just as sin affects all people, God's offer of salvation includes all people (3:23-24). The first half of the letter answers the deep problem of idolatry described in 1:18-23, a problem especially relevant to Gentiles. The Jews, however, have their own particular problem of spiritual pride, described in 2:4-5. After reaching the high point of 8:38-39, that nothing can separate us from God's love in Christ Jesus, one might wonder about the historical question of why Israel has rejected this gracious plan of salvation in Jesus Christ. Are the promises

God made to Israel as his chosen people long ago (Exod. 19:5-6) still valid?

Paul shows through the exposition of Scripture that the gospel has been part of God's plan since the beginning. "Since it was in Holy Scripture that God had announced his plans for the 'last days,' it is in Holy Scripture that the justification of God's ways with Gentiles and Israel must be found."[3] The key question for interpretation is, How does Paul appeal to Scripture to show that God has not abandoned Israel and that the promises are still true? Why have the people of Israel failed to see these promises in their own Scriptures?

The Use of Scripture in Romans 9–11

These chapters form a clear unit in the letter, with a clear beginning and end.[4] This part of the letter can be neatly divided by Paul's rhetorical questions, with an introductory personal lament (9:1-5) and a closing doxology (11:33-36). Each section builds on ideas from the previous sections.[5]

Paul's Great Anguish over Israel's Failure (Rom. 9:1-5)

Romans 9 begins with an abrupt shift in tone from the highpoint of 8:39. This section begins with Paul expressing his sorrow for the poor response of his people, Israel, to the gospel of Jesus Christ. In spite of all of their privileges (adoption, glory, covenants, law, worship, promises, patriarchs, the Messiah [9:4-5]), they have rejected Jesus. Their privileges have failed to provide them with the righteousness they seek. These verses set up the implied critical issue of this part of the letter: Why has Israel not believed in Jesus as the Messiah? Paul's deep love for his people and

---

3. William M. Greathouse, with George Lyons, *Romans 9–16*, New Beacon Bible Commentary (Kansas City: Beacon Hill Press of Kansas City, 2008), 44.

4. James D. G. Dunn, *Romans 9–16*, Word Biblical Commentary (Dallas: Word Books, 2002), 518.

5. Douglas J. Moo, *The Epistle to the Romans*, The New International Commentary on the New Testament (Grand Rapids: Eerdmans, 1996), 553-54.

his commitment to preach the gospel to them set a positive tone for what follows, in spite of the deeply divisive topic of God's rejection of Israel.

God's Sovereign, Merciful, and Inclusive Grace (Rom. 9:6-29)

The next unit begins with the assertion that the word of God has not failed in spite of Israel's rejection of God's promised Messiah (v. 6a). This "word" contains the promises just given in verses 4-5 and likely refers to Old Testament Scripture, which is the primary source of God's promises to Israel. Paul will appeal especially to these promises to support his ideas in these chapters. This assertion suggests that he extensively uses the Old Testament in this part of the letter because it is the sacred container of the promises claimed by Israel and the promises Jesus fulfilled.

Paul's next statement sets the stage for the coming confrontation with the unbelieving Jews. He claims that there is a difference between ethnic Israel and spiritual Israel. "Israel" is a key term in these chapters. It occurs eleven times in chapters 9–11 but nowhere else in the letter. Being biological descendants of Abraham does not guarantee salvation (9:6b-7). Not all who claim Abraham as their father are part of the true Israel, but only those who believe (4:1-16). The new people of God are defined not by ethnicity but by faith. This claim sets the stage for the first quotation of Scripture from Genesis 21:12 in Romans 9:7. In the original context of Genesis 21, God reminds Abraham that the promise will come through Isaac and not Ishmael. Physical descent is not the final determining factor in receiving the promise, but God's merciful decision is. Paul "interprets" this verse, using the style of *pesher* (eschatological fulfillment), to establish the basic principle that there is a difference between children of flesh and children of promise. Only those who are children of the promise are part of Israel, and those children participate in this promise through faith (Rom. 4:13). Paul is preparing for his crucial point that God's grace is inclusive for all who believe. Paul clarifies in Romans 9:9 what he means by the "promise" by quoting the key idea from Genesis 18:10, 14: the elderly and barren Sarah would have a son in fulfillment of the promises God made to Abraham in Genesis 17:15-16.

Paul offers no further commentary but moves on to the next generation in Israel's history to add more support for his basic claim that the promise comes not through blood or birthright but through God's gracious election. In Romans 9:10-13, Paul compares the two sons of Isaac. Even though Esau was a son by blood, it was through the younger Jacob that God carried out his promise. To add weight to this point, Paul claims that God's election was "before the twins were born or had done anything good or bad" (v. 11). In verse 12, he quotes Genesis 25:23, using it in its literal sense, to show that physical descent ("works") was not enough to be part of the promise. God's election is confirmed further by a quote from Malachi 1:2-3 in Romans 9:13, which uses the first person "I loved . . . I hated . . ." In the original context of Malachi, this refers to two nations (see Gen 25:23*a*), Israel and Edom. There is no need to be specific in the context of Romans 9, since the point about God's choice of Jacob and his descendants is clear.

Beginning in verse 14 with the question "What then shall we say?" Paul takes up a potential objection, one which modern readers may also raise: if God can choose who receives mercy, then is God "unrighteous" or "unfair"? Paul answers this question with the strong "By no means!" and then cites Exodus 33:19 (using the Septuagint) to clarify what he means. This verse records God's response to Moses's plea to experience God's glory. Paul quotes here the part of God's response to Moses that reveals one aspect of God's essential, righteous nature: God is merciful and compassionate. Paul follows this up in Romans 9:16 with a principle he finds in the Exodus verse: receiving God's mercy is dependent upon God and not any human effort, wish, or decision. This assertion is an echo of what Paul wrote earlier in the letter about God's universal offer of grace. If this offer were dependent upon human ability to choose God, then no one would be qualified to ask for it because of the problem of sin (Rom. 3:23-24). "If God does anything at all for sinful humans, it is out of his mercy. If he does nothing, he is not unjust, for we deserve nothing."[6] Paul knows that the offer of salvation must come totally from God's side. Salvation is always a matter of God's grace. God can choose to show mercy to whomever he wishes.

Romans 9:17 adds further proof by citing Exodus 9:16 from the story of Pharaoh's refusal to release the Hebrew slaves. Although this citation is not exactly what is in the Hebrew Masoretic Text or the Greek Septuagint, Paul captures the key point of the original context. God's sovereignty was on display in this conflict with Pharaoh. There is never any doubt in the original story that God was in control, since God told Moses from the start that God would later harden Pharaoh's heart (4:21). This hardening was in response to Pharaoh's refusal to heed God's offer of mercy (7:13). The hardening of Pharaoh's heart contrasts with God's offer of mercy and salvation (vv. 3-5). Israel of Paul's day faced the same situation. If the people of Israel refused the offer of God's mercy, they would also experience a hardening of their hearts, with the final outcome for them being that they would better see God's offer of mercy (Rom. 11:5-7, 25).

Like the earlier quotation, Paul follows this up with a principle introduced with "therefore" (9:18). God is not bound by what people think. This is a strong warning for any Jews who were operating under the false assumption of security in their heritage or bloodline. God will act consistently with what he has revealed in Scripture about himself. In other words, God sets his own standard for mercy and grace. This does not rule

---

6. Greathouse, with Lyons, *Romans 9–16*, 58.

out the human need for the response of faith—since that need is clear in other passages (see 10:9-13)—but highlights its urgency even more.

Paul next takes up a question that a thoughtful person may have: if God is totally sovereign, can we resist him (9:19)? Paul turns the question around with an accusatory question: "But who are you, a human being, to talk back to God?" (v. 20). To answer that question, Paul again turns to Scripture, using the metaphor of a clay pot and the potter who makes it. He quotes from Isaiah 29:16 and then possibly alludes to Isaiah 45:9, with the idea of the clay rejecting the will of the potter (see also Jer. 18:1-6, with a possible echo of Wis. 15:7). His rhetorical question in Romans 9:21 shows that this is impossible and even absurd. The assumed conclusion reflects the points made earlier: God as the potter can do as he desires and purposes, with the ultimate outcome being the display of his glory before the world. Verse 22 moves on to apply the Scriptural illustration (marked in Greek with *de* [now], which is untranslated in the NIV) with a long conditional sentence ending with verse 24. The basic point he makes here is that God has been patient with Israel's apostasy in order to show the extent of his mercy. The final outcome of God's sovereign mercy will be that his glory will be seen by all, both Jews and Gentiles. God's patience with Israel has allowed the Gentiles to come to faith.

Paul next quotes a rapid series of four Old Testament passages to build on his key point in verse 24, that both Jews and Gentiles are the targets of God's mercy. The people of God are defined by God's call and mercy and not by hereditary or national identity. These verses can be read with this direct application in the background. The source of these quotations is unclear, with a mixture from the Hebrew Masoretic Text, the Greek Septuagint, and possibly memory. For example, Paul changes "I will say" in the original Hosea 2:23 with "I will call," which seems to make God "choosing" the objects of his mercy in Romans 9:23. These selections are united in the form of *gezerah shawah*,[7] where the linked words are related to the identity of God's people:

Rom. 9:25 from Hos. 2:23:	my people
	my loved one
Rom. 9:26 from Hos. 1:10:	my people
	children of the living God
Rom. 9:27-28 from Isa. 10:22-23	Israelites
	remnant
Rom. 9:29 from Isa. 1:9	descendants

One critical issue when examining these references is the identity of "my people." Since these people were once not God's people, Paul is likely applying Hosea 2:23 to the Gentiles and incorporating them into God's people. This agrees with what he wrote to the Galatians, that "there is neither Jew nor Greek . . . for [we] are all one in Christ Jesus" (Gal. 3:28). Sadly, as Isaiah 10:22-23 shows, only a few Israelites, "the remnant," have responded to God's offer of salvation in Jesus Christ (Rom. 9:27). That is the real issue in these chapters: Why have only a few responded, and what about the rest? The quote from Isaiah 1:9 implies that God has chosen to work through Gentiles because if he relied on the Jews, only a few people in the world would be saved (Rom. 9:29). God's love is for the whole world (John 3:16). His grace is for all people. His rejection of Israel is based on Israel's rejection of Jesus Christ.

Why Israel Has Been Rejected (Rom. 9:30–10:21)

After establishing the greatness of God's sovereign mercy, Paul takes up the problem of why the people of Israel have rejected Jesus as their

---

7. This is number two of the aforementioned seven rules of interpretation used by Hillel. Here, passages with the same or similar words are given analogous meanings or applications. *Jewish Encyclopedia*, s.v. "Rules of Hillel, the Seven," by Wilhelm Bacher and Jacob Zallel Lauterbach, accessed September 28, 2021, https://www.jewishencyclopedia.com/articles/12936-rules-of-hillel-the-seven.

Messiah by asking another rhetorical question. The key question following from Romans 9:29 is, On what basis are the Gentiles included and Jews excluded from salvation (vv. 30-31)? Gentiles have responded to God's righteousness found in Christ by believing, while the Jews have continued in their misunderstanding of God's plan. By the end of this chapter, Paul demonstrates that God's plan is clearly given in Scripture; therefore, the Jews have no excuse for their rejection.

The key words in this passage are "faith" (vv. 30, 32) and "righteousness" (vv. 30, 31), both of which are the focus of 1:16-17 and used in key places throughout the letter. Believing in Jesus is the only way by which God's grace is able to make people right before God and conform them to the righteous mind of Christ (3:21–4:25; 12:1-2). By this point in the letter, the Roman believers should have a clear understanding of this basic principle. The problem is that the Jews are ignorant of it and do not know the true way to righteousness (10:2, 3). They are stuck in their misguided and wrong understanding. Paul emphasizes their problem with three overlapping phrases: (1) they "pursued the law as the way of righteousness" (9:31), (2) "as if it were by works" (v. 32), and (3) "sought to establish their own" righteousness (10:3). All of these focus on human effort instead of God's grace. Such effort is the result of pride and misguided zeal (2:5, 8).

In Romans 9:33 Paul combines two passages from Isaiah—8:14 and 28:16—to add support to this claim. He may be drawing upon a common early Christian interpretation of these Old Testament passages (Matt. 21:42; Mark 12:10; Luke 20:17; Acts 4:11; 1 Pet. 2:7). These quotations do not match exactly the original Isaiah texts but are a conflation of the verses. Both original verses contain the word "stone," so Paul may be using a form of *gezerah shawah* to link the verses. He could also be using *binyan ab mi-shene ketubim*[8] to join the two verses together to form the one principle centered on accepting or rejecting the stone. The "stone" or "rock" is not identified in Romans 9:33, but the later context of 10:9 implies that it is Jesus Christ. Jews from Qumran before Paul's time had already identified this stone to be the Messiah (1QH 6:26-27; 1QS 8:7), which suggests that this idea was already in Jewish thinking. If so, Paul and the early Christians only needed to apply this interpretation to Christ.

Paul's application appears in the phrases he chooses from Isaiah. On the one hand, as Isaiah 8:14 warns, the stone will cause Israel to stumble and fall. On the other hand, as Isaiah 28:16 promises, believing in the same stone removes shame and provides a sure foundation for life. The people of Israel stumbled over Christ because it required that they humble themselves as sinners before God and accept his grace through Christ (Rom. 2:1–3:20).[9] Their failure to believe in Christ was predicted in Scripture, but as Romans 10–11 will show, this is not a permanent rejection, because there is always hope for those who believe. Paul restates this hope in 10:1: "My heart's desire and prayer to God for the Israelites is that they may be saved." He will lay out the way of salvation in Romans 10 and use Scripture to support it.

Chapter 10 continues the comparison of the two approaches to righteousness that underlie much of the discussion in this letter and are specifically described in 9:30-32. Paul's focus is especially on unbelieving Jews. He uses Scripture quotations to support the gospel and offers unbelieving Jews a reason for putting their faith in Jesus. It is a wide-open invitation "for everyone who believes" (10:4).

One of the fundamental issues Paul demonstrates is that the Jews misunderstood their own Scriptures. His eyes were opened through

---

8. Hillel's fourth rule of interpretation, which holds that a principle "generalized from two . . . passages" can pertain to other related passages. Ibid.

9. Greathouse, with Lyons, *Romans 9–16*, 71.

a revelation on the road to Damascus. The majority of Jews remained blinded, as he was (1 Tim. 1:13), in their pursuit of righteousness by following the traditions and interpretations of their elders. Paul had a new hermeneutic of Scripture that was formed by his experience of the risen Jesus Christ. He saw faith in God's mercy shown on the cross as the only way to righteousness. The Jews tried to establish their own righteousness by following the law, but this approach was misguided and out of ignorance (Rom. 10:3) and only led to defeat (7:14-24). The problem was not the law, which is "holy, righteous and good" (v. 12), but trying to obtain God's righteousness through human effort in keeping the law (3:20, 27-28; 4:2; 8:3-4). Christ puts an end to this self-righteousness and makes righteousness available to anyone who believes (10:4). This allows the law to serve in its rightful role as the guide leading to Christ (Gal. 3:19, 24) by convicting of sin and showing our need for God's grace in Christ. Obedience to the law does not make a person righteous, but following it is the proper response of those who have been made righteous through the blood of Christ. At the heart of this "obedience of faith" is the command to love (Rom. 13:9; Gal. 5:14).

> **Paul saw faith in God's mercy shown on the cross as the only way to righteousness.**

Paul uses a series of Old Testament quotations from the Israelites' own sacred text to help them overcome their ignorance about God's plan of salvation. He begins in Romans 10:5 with an appeal to Moses, quoting Leviticus 18:5. We can view this verse in two ways. One is that Paul may be setting up a contrast between what Moses says and what came later in the gospel, thus resulting in a law-gospel dichotomy. Many in the church since the Reformation have followed this line of thinking.[10] This would

---

10. Moo, *Romans*, 644.

account for the Jews' confusion about the law and righteousness. However, it places Moses, and thus Scripture, in a bad light and makes what God says in Scripture inconsistent. Another way to view this quotation is to see it as an intentional contradiction, as a quotation the Jews might use to justify their thinking that righteousness comes through obedience to the law. Paul has already shown that this is impossible; because of the power of sin, no one can keep the law well enough to be considered righteous (Rom. 1:18–3:20). Paul uses *pesher*[11] to contrast the Jews' faulty interpretation with how his Christological hermeneutic answers their dilemma and is also consistent with the whole tenor of the Old Testament.

Next, in Romans 10:6-8, Paul asks a series of questions taken from Deuteronomy 30:12-14, with a short preface possibly from Deuteronomy 9:4. The NIV displays Paul's *pesher* interpretation of Deuteronomy by putting his ideas in parentheses (Gk. simply has "that is"). His gloss gives the passage "a clear messianic and soteriological significance."[12] Paul connects Deuteronomy to key events in Jesus's life: his ascension-exaltation and death-resurrection. Paul uses the series of questions to show how the Old Testament is fulfilled in the gospel, "the message concerning faith that we proclaim" (Rom. 10:8).

Verses 9-10 show how this word of faith leads to salvation. There are two key activities from Deuteronomy 30:14 that show how one must embrace the gospel. Paul connects the "mouth" with the key confession that "Jesus is Lord," and the "heart" to believing Jesus rose from the dead (Rom. 10:9; the key idea in 1:4). God wants people to change allegiance from self and sin and affirm his sovereignty by proclaiming Jesus to be Lord (6:1-13; Phil. 2:9-11). This inner response and outer confession show that salvation is not difficult to obtain and does not require someone to keep

---

11. Greathouse, with Lyons, *Romans 9–16*, 77.
12. Ibid., 78.

a set of laws. Paul affirms this idea in Romans 10:11 by quoting Isaiah 28:16 again (see Rom. 9:33). This quotation is linked to verses 9 and 10 by the word "believe." Using this verse here implies that salvation removes any fear of shame at the final judgment, something the Jews would face because of their spiritual pride unless they repented and believed in Jesus as the Messiah (2:5). Paul is showing that the way to salvation is open to all who believe. The wall between Jews and Gentiles has been removed in Christ (10:12; Gal. 3:28; Eph. 2:13-18), because everyone must make the same confession of faith. Paul emphasizes this even more with a quotation from Joel 2:32 in Romans 10:13. This verse was important in the early Christian witness to Christ, as demonstrated by Peter quoting the same verse on the day of Pentecost in Acts 2:21.

Paul likewise uses this verse to move into an appeal to the readers—and in particular to the Jews—to respond to this simple message. Paul builds on the word "calls" from Joel 2:32 by using a stair-step series of connected rhetorical questions, each beginning with "how can" (Rom. 10:14-15). In order to believe, people must hear the gospel. To hear, someone needs to preach it to them. The final factor is that the preacher must be sent. Paul ends the series in verse 15 with a shortened quotation from Isaiah 52:7. He may have in mind the context (possibly like the rabbinic *dabar ha-lamed me-'inyano*)[13] of the Isaiah passage, since God had sent prophets to call Israel back to covenantal faithfulness. Historically, God sent Paul to both Jews and Gentiles (Rom. 1:5, 14, 16). Paul faithfully preached the gospel wherever he went. This letter is a form of preaching and serves as an open invitation for unbelieving Jews to hear the gospel and respond because "now is the day of salvation" (2 Cor. 6:2). This puts the obligation on them to respond to his letter. They have no more excuse for ignorance,

---

13. Hillel's seventh rule uses context to interpret a passage. *Jewish Encyclopedia*, s.v. "Rules of Hillel, the Seven."

because they have now heard the right way of salvation, which is by faith and confession.

This might be why Paul proceeds to consider, in Romans 10:16-21, why some Israelites refuse to believe, by quoting a question from Isaiah 53:1. At first, this quotation seems to take a verse out of context, but Isaiah 53 begins with the same theme of people refusing to accept the messenger God sends. This adds further weight to the accusation that the Jews are not listening to God. Romans 10:17 now makes the link and logic clear by providing the principle that connects Israel's Scripture to the gospel. The message proclaimed to Israel is the "word about Christ."

Paul's rhetorical question in verse 18 makes explicit that the Israelites have no excuse to continue in ignorance, because they have heard the gospel through Paul or other preachers. He presents a series of Old Testament quotations in verses 18-21 (in the form of *gezerah shawah*) as more scriptural evidence to confront the Jews with their need to make a decision about Jesus. He quotes Psalm 19:4 in Romans 10:18 to show that God's revelation "has gone out into all the earth," implying that many people have heard and had the opportunity to respond to the gospel. The language here is hyperbolic but supports Paul's claim that the invitation is open to all people, regardless of ethnicity or religious background.

Paul's next rhetorical question in verse 19 further pressures the Jews to accept the gospel because now they are without excuse; even Scripture predicted their refusal to believe. Because they had heard and understood the message of the gospel, the responsibility was on them and not the preacher. The quotation of Deuteronomy 32:21 shows that God knew Israel would fail to believe and that this would open the door to other nations. In the original context in Deuteronomy, God was jealous of Israel's idolatry and so would make Israel jealous of God's inclusion of another "nation" (Gk., *ethnei*, often translated as "Gentile"). Paul makes a specific connection to the Israel of his day by changing the pronoun "them" in the original to "you" in his quotation. He will develop the idea of Israel's jealousy of the Gentiles more in Romans 11.

With the final quotation in this chapter, Paul turns from the Law to the Prophets by quoting Isaiah 65:1-2 in Romans 10:20-21. This quotation emphasizes the point made earlier that Israel's refusal to listen to God would result in God turning to the Gentiles. Isaiah 65:1 in its original context is addressed to Israel, but Paul uses an analogy to connect this to the Gentiles. This connection may be aided by Isaiah's reference to "nations" in the Septuagint, which is the part of the verse Paul leaves out. The next verse returns to Isaiah's emphasis upon the Israelites' failure to follow God and their choice instead to pursue "their own imaginations" (Isa. 65:2). The problem that remains is that Israel is a "disobedient and obstinate people" (Rom. 10:21). With the issue of ignorance resolved, the remaining problem is the refusal to believe. Paul will show next how even this is part of God's plan.

Appeal to Gentiles (Rom. 11:1-10)

Since God has included the Gentiles in the plan of salvation, Paul begins Romans 11 with the next logical question: Has God then rejected Israel? Paul again answers with the strong negation, "By no means!" (v. 1). First Samuel 12:22 and Psalm 94:14 may stand behind this question[14] and affirm God's election of Israel. Paul's own life testifies that God has not rejected the Jews. The problem is not that God has rejected Israel but that Israel has refused to listen to God. Paul advances his argument in this chapter by answering rhetorical questions with Scripture.

---

14. Greathouse, with Lyons, *Romans 9–16*, 91.

His first point is that God has reserved a faithful remnant chosen by grace. To support this, he quotes from the story of Elijah in 1 Kings 19:10, 18. He assumes the readers are familiar with this story by his asking rhetorically, "Don't you know what Scripture says?" (Rom. 11:2). He modifies the quotation to emphasize "the divine initiative in preserving the faithfulness of the elect minority."[15] He uses the interpretive method of analogy, marked in verse 5 by the phrase "so too, at the present time," to show the similarity of the remnant of Elijah's day with the believing Jews of Paul's day. Paul returns to the theme of Romans 9 by emphasizing in 11:5b-6 that this remnant is chosen by grace and not by "works," which represent the human effort to be righteous by the law. For salvation to be by grace, it must come from God's side and not humanity's. God is free to give his grace to whomever he chooses, and so God has chosen all people (11:32). The only way to participate in this grace is through faith, and therein lies the problem for Israel—a lack of faith. The remnant is defined "by their absolute dependence on God's grace."[16]

The difficult question of verse 7 is the identity of the "elect." The context of Romans indicates that the elect are Gentiles and Jews who believe in Jesus Christ. Conversely, Gentiles and Jews who refuse to believe will receive God's wrath (1:18; 2:5; 3:5), experienced as rejection and hardening of the heart (1:24, 26, 28; 2:8, 9). Paul applies 11:7 to unbelieving Jews and supports it with a catena of citations from all three parts of Jewish Scripture: Law, Prophets, and Writings. The string of quotations could be *binyan ab mi-shene ketubim*, where all these passages are used to support Paul's new principle that God's rejection of the Israelites is due to their refusal to believe in his word. There is also a verbal link in the style of

---

15. Ibid., 92.
16. Ibid., 93.

charaz (pearl stringing),[17] with the common concept of "eyes" that cannot see what God is doing. Paul combines parts of Deuteronomy 29:4 and Isaiah 29:10—both of which refer to dull minds, eyes, and ears—to show that this hardening is part of God's plan. Later, in Romans 11:25-27, we learn that this was to give the Gentiles the opportunity to hear the gospel. Just as the ancient Israelites could not understand the depth of God's grace toward them in giving them the Land of Promise, so the Jews of Paul's day could not see God's grace in Jesus Christ. Paul continues the "dull senses" theme by quoting Psalm 69:22-23 in Romans 11:9-10. In the original context, this is a curse against David's enemies. The same kind of curse awaits unbelieving Jews.

Israel's Hardening Is Not Permanent (Rom. 11:11-32)

Paul asks another rhetorical question to show that God intends the Israelites' stumbling to be only temporary, and their hardening can be remedied through the gospel because their transgressions (v. 11) can be forgiven. Their refusal has provided an opportunity for the Gentiles to hear the gospel. The Israelites' hardening will ultimately lead to their salvation because of the grace of God. Meanwhile, however, it would be easy to conclude that the Gentiles have replaced Israel in God's favor and plan (v. 12). Paul turns his focus to the Gentiles in this section and warns them against this assumption (v. 13). He uses a form of *qal wa-homer* (from the lesser to the greater)[18] in verses 12, 15-16 to compare the greatness of the Gentiles' experience of salvation to the even more significant salvation of hardened Israel, who should have had insight already into God's plan in

---

17. Like stringing pearls, *charaz* was a style of rabbinic preaching that strung one "like-sounding, or really similar," passage to another. Alfred Edersheim, *The Life and Times of Jesus the Messiah*, 8th ed. (London: Longmans, Green, 1907), 1:449. See William Barclay, *The Letter to the Romans*, The New Daily Study Bible (Louisville, KY: Westminster John Knox Press, 2002), 64.

18. This is Hillel's first rule of interpretation, which states that what applies to a lesser situation will apply to a greater situation. Michael H. Burer, "Focus on Rabbinic Exegesis," *Exegesis for Christ, the Gospel, and the Church* (blog), WordPress.com, https://michaelhburer.wordpress.com/2012/07/09/focus-on-rabbinic-exegesis/.

Scripture. If the Israelites' hardening brought salvation to the Gentiles, how much more blessing would their salvation bring? Unbelieving Israel will finally realize its problem and come to faith in Christ. The way of salvation is not different for Israel or anybody else (see Eph. 2:4-9).

The mixed metaphors in Romans 11:16 could be an allusion to Numbers 15:17-21 and the offering of the first grain or dough. The basic principle is that the holiness of the first part of the dough guaranteed the holiness of the whole batch. Another possible background is Leviticus 19:23-25, which states that the first harvest of fruit trees is to be given as a praise offering to the Lord. Holiness in this context has the cultic sense of dedicating something to God (see Exod. 29:37). Jewish believers as the remnant and Gentile believers are the firstfruits that guarantee the full harvest will come in.

Paul builds on the image of root and branches from Romans 11:16 to introduce the allegory of the olive tree in verse 17. Behind this image may be the image of Israel as an olive tree found in Jeremiah 11:16 and Hosea 14:6. In Romans 11:17-24, the olive tree represents the true Israel of faith, the people of God who live by faith. Believing Gentiles are grafted in, believing Jews remain part of it, but unbelieving Jews are cut off. They may be made of olive wood (hereditary) but are not children of promise unless they believe. The key is faith by which both believing Jews and Gentiles become the spiritual descendants of Abraham (ch. 4; 8:16). The church does not replace Israel but continues what God started long ago. Paul uses this image to warn Gentile believers in 11:19-21 not to get prideful because of their inclusion in the people of God, but there is also an implied warning to the unbelieving Jews. God does not arbitrarily condemn certain people; condemnation comes only in response to the decision to reject the light of Christ. "One's standing before God is provisional,"[19] dependent upon faith and God's kindness (v. 22). God's condemnation of Israel is provisional, and he will "graft . . . in again" those who believe (v. 23). Faith is the key factor in being part of the olive tree. "Despite what God *can* do, the human response of faith/unbelief is decisive in determining what he *will* do."[20] Another *qal wa-homer* comparison appears in verse 24 to show how great the salvation of Israel would be. The phrase "contrary to nature" indicates that God's grace is able to graft both wild and natural branches into the olive tree; both Gentiles and Jews can be included in the one people of God because of God's mercy (ch. 9).

Romans 11:25-26 summarizes Paul's prayer that all Israel will be saved, but meanwhile, the Gentiles must not become proud of their salvation. It is difficult to know what he means by "all Israel" in verse 26, but this at least expresses his deep hope and confidence in God's plan of redemption and fulfillment of ancient scriptural promises. To support this and show how Israel will be saved, he quotes Isaiah 59:20-21 in Romans 11:26-27*a* and a phrase from Isaiah 27:9 in Romans 11:27*b*. He

> **The Israelites must come to know the depth of their sin so that they can seek God's forgiveness.**

changes the original text of Isaiah 59:20 to read, "The deliverer will come *from* Zion" (emphasis added). The "deliverer" in the Isaianic context is Yahweh. Paul could have in mind here that Messiah Jesus will come from Zion to deliver the Israelites and fulfill God's covenant with them, possibly an allusion to the second coming. Paul may draw upon Isaiah 27 because of its reference to the removal of sins as part of the new covenant (see Jer. 31:34). All the people of Israel will eventually be saved because they will finally come to faith, which will fulfill God's promise to Abraham (Rom. 11:28-29). Verse 31 suggests that the testimony of the Gentiles' salvation will lead to the salvation of Israel. Paul's conclusion is that

19. Greathouse, with Lyons, *Romans 9–16*, 106.
20. Ibid., 107.

God has definitely not rejected the Israelites but wants to extend mercy to them. They must come to know the depth of their sin so that they can seek God's forgiveness (v. 32). "The OT refers to God's character as holy love and his gracious purpose to save all humanity as constant and unchanging."[21]

Hymn of Praise (Rom. 11:33-36)

After thinking so deeply about God's mercy and intention for all to be saved, Paul bursts forth with a doxology. He quotes two Old Testament texts to emphasize the mystery of God's purposes and methods. He uses the Septuagint version of Isaiah 40:13 in Romans 11:34. The Hebrew text reads, "Who can measure the Spirit of the LORD?" (AT), and the Septuagint has, "Who can know the mind of the Lord?" (AT). Romans 11:35 paraphrases the first line of Job 41:11, changing the first-person pronoun "I" to "God." Both quotations are questions that reinforce Paul's wonder about God and must be answered: No one can know "the depth of the riches of the wisdom and knowledge of God! How unsearchable his judgments, and his paths beyond tracing out!" (Rom. 11:33). The final statement ends the whole section of Romans 9–11 with a word of praise and glory to this awesome and merciful God (11:36).

Romans 9–11 in Contemporary Context

Looking at the quotations and allusions to the Old Testament helps us navigate a challenging section of this letter. Paul's use of Scripture is varied and not always easy to understand. It is clear that he sees the church, made of believing Jews and Gentiles, as the fulfillment of God's plan for ancient Israel. It is also just as clear that Paul's faith in the promises of Scripture possessed a strong confidence that ethnic Jews would one day come to

---

21. Ibid., 117.

believe in Jesus as their Messiah. He had at his disposal a significant memory of texts to fit his purpose. It is impossible to tell if he had scrolls of the Old Testament with him (2 Tim. 4:13) or if his memory was prodigious and he could recall what he had spent a lifetime studying. We can discern several important insights from Romans 9–11 that compel us to follow Paul's desired path for those in his day.

First, in these chapters, Paul in many ways saves the Old Testament for the church. He shows there is continuity between the Old Testament and the New Testament in the witness of salvation through Jesus Christ. Jesus fulfills the promises God made through the Patriarchs, the Law, the Prophets, and the Writings. There is theological unity between the Testaments. Christians of today can read the whole Bible with confidence, knowing that God had a big plan since the beginning. Like the early church, we can see the seeds of the gospel in the Old Testament.

The implications of this are significant for biblical theology. Paul's emphasis upon God's mercy and grace throughout Romans helps us realize anew that God as revealed in the Old Testament is also merciful and gracious. This vision of God is apparent in his plan to include Gentiles as part of his people. The church fulfills the plans God had for Israel (Exod. 19:5-6; 1 Pet. 2:9-10). God's promises to Israel as a people will be fulfilled, but this fulfillment will be consistent with God's revelation of grace in Jesus Christ. The people of God are defined by faith in Christ, not ethnicity. We must be careful of arrogance lest we think that the Gentile church today can leave out the descendants of Abraham by birth. It is through the church's witness that Jews will come to believe in their Messiah. The corporate election of Israel is still dependent upon faith. There is only one olive tree and one way to be grafted into it. Paul helps us have a clear vision of who the people of God are.

Second, faith is the critical response needed to participate in God's gracious offer of salvation. The mysterious combination of God's grace and the human freedom to choose in faith to receive this grace is what is required. "God is able to work with all things to achieve his ultimate purposes without violating human freedom to persist in unbelief, come to faith, or persist in faith."[22] Paul shows that this optimism in God's grace has been present since the patriarchs and the giving of the promises to Abraham. Faith is not meritorious but responsive. God's plan of salvation is not dependent on human effort or ability to keep commandments but only on the mercy shown on the cross. "God's mercy is absolutely sovereign, which means that salvation is entirely a matter of grace rather than any form of human achievement."[23] The fundamental decision one must make is to remain in disobedience or to trust in God's mercy. Like the Jews of Paul's day, many people today have a fundamental misunderstanding of righteousness. They think that if their good deeds outweigh their bad ones, they will make it to heaven. Paul shows in these chapters and throughout the letter that this thinking is flawed and will result in hearts hardened with pride and will ultimately bring judgment.

Third, these chapters help us deal with the sticky issue of the doctrine of election. There is never any question about God's sovereign mercy. Some interpreters, particularly in the Reformed tradition, see in these verses support for the doctrine of double predestination, that God ordains some to be saved and some to be lost.[24] This, in my opinion and interpretation, is a misreading of these chapters. Paul is writing about the fate of Israel in these chapters and not individuals. The plan of salvation is an open invitation for all to participate. Grace has the upper hand: "It

---

22. Ibid., 108.

23. Robert Jewett, *Romans: A Commentary*, Hermeneia (Minneapolis: Fortress Press, 2007), 710.

24. See *The Westminster Confession of Faith*, ch. 3, arts. 6, 7, with introduction and notes by John Macpherson (Edinburgh: T. and T. Clark, 1882), 49-51, https://archive.org/details/westminsterconf00unknuoft/page/n3/mode/2up.

comes to those who do not deserve it ([Rom.] 3:22-24; 5:8-10), it is more abundant than sin (5:20-21) and breaks its power (6:22; 7:6), and there is nothing anywhere that can thwart it (8:38-39)."[25] Sin and the refusal to respond to grace only highlight more the significance of God's mercy. The hardening of which Paul writes is for the specific purpose of helping Israel see the futility of the life of sin and unbelief. God's grace is free for all, even the Jews who have been cut off from the olive tree of God's people. There is always the opportunity to return and be grafted back in. Wesley taught that "according to this, all true believers are in Scripture termed elect, as all who continue in unbelief are so long properly reprobates, that is, unapproved of God, and without discernment touching the things of the Spirit."[26] The doctrine of prevenient grace shows that God gives grace to all, but not all allow that grace to work in their lives and bring them to the place where they embrace saving grace.

---

25. Paul J. Achtemeier, *Romans*, Interpretation: A Bible Commentary for Teaching and Preaching (Atlanta: John Knox Press, 1985), 163.

26. John Wesley, "Predestination Calmly Considered," in *The Works of John Wesley*, ed. Thomas Jackson, 3rd ed. (London: Wesleyan Methodist Book Room, 1872; repr., Peabody, MA: Hendrickson, 1984), 10:210.

6

Moral Exhortation
1 CORINTHIANS 6:12-20

Paul's Agenda

Paul's letters have many directives for how believers should act. These directions are given mostly in the form of commands, usually using the second person plural, "you all," since he was writing to churches. In some commands, he includes himself, using "let us." Commands in themselves do not constitute a separate literary genre, since they are contained in just about every major genre within the Bible. A statement can be easily formed into a command in most languages. However, the way Paul writes the commands in his letters serves as part of his rhetorical strategy to convince the readers to follow a better way of life. Thus it is helpful to give them special attention in our study of interpreting his letters.

Paraenesis is the term for exhortation often used to address moral issues. This form of exhortation contains expectations of proper behavior and warnings about bad behavior. Paraenesis often reminds people of something they already should know. Paraenesis can be found in vice and virtue lists, household codes, and directions for how believers should live in their cultural setting.

Paul uses paraenesis in his letters in three ways. First, he deals with specific, actual, or potential problems made known to him by letter, word of mouth, or his own knowledge of a situation. He urges churches and individuals to stop living according to the ways of the world and to begin living according to the paradigm of being *in Christ*. Second, his exhortation is built on the theological foundation of Jesus's death and resurrection. Third, he supports and illustrates this foundation with his own life and example. As a steward of the divine "mysteries" (1 Cor. 4:1), he serves as an example of this new life in Christ (v. 16; 11:1).

There are several strategies to use in interpreting the moral exhortations in Paul's letters. First, as with all of Scripture, it is important to address textual matters, such as literary context, grammar, syntax, and key words. Second, because ethics usually deal with behavior and relationships with other people, it is helpful to explore social and cultural issues that reveal the application of the principles guiding the exhortations. Third, because Paul's ethics express faith in Christ through obedience in everyday situations, identifying the connection to Paul's doctrine of Christ can lead us to the timeless truths that apply to our situations today.

Paul's moral exhortations are never isolated but are always found in the context of his theology. This is evident in his use of the Greek verb, which reveals a lot about Paul's approach to ethics. The Greek verb can be formed into four "moods." Mood is how a verb expresses action—that is, as an actuality or a probability. The *indicative* mood is used for statements of fact or basic description; a majority of verbs in the New Testament are in this form. Paul uses the indicative when he reflects on what God has done through the life, death, and resurrection of Jesus Christ.

The *imperative* mood is used for commands or rules, particularly for how people should act. Paul's letters have many commands, especially related to expected behavior. Significantly, these commands are usually given in the context of theological statements in the indicative. In other words, morality (human obedience shown through holy behavior) is made possible because of grace (the change God makes in the human condition). Anytime interpreters study one of Paul's moral exhortations, they should also look for the theological foundation upon which this exhortation is built. This almost always will be in the nearby context and sometimes even in the same sentence.

Challenges in Corinth

In Paul's first canonical letter to the Corinthian church (he wrote at least one earlier letter, which is lost; see 1 Cor. 5:9), he mainly gives attention to correcting improper attitudes and actions and provides a good example of moral exhortation. First Corinthians can be neatly divided into several sections. Chapters 1–4 form the first major section, within which Paul lays out the fundamental spiritual issues that will appear in the specific moral exhortations of the rest of the letter.

Beginning in 1:18, Paul lays out the theological foundation for all the moral, church, and theological issues that he addresses in the rest of the letter. He clearly reminds them of his core message found in the cross of Christ (2:1-5). The cross reveals the very power and wisdom of God, even though it looks foolish and weak to unbelievers (1:18-25). Through the cross, God brings about a new age with a new way of life consistent with the way of the cross (v. 30). Paul shows that the way to spiritual maturity comes not in relying upon human ability but in relying upon the Holy Spirit to guide and reveal God's plan through the divine mystery of Christ. Maturity (*teleios*; 2:6) comes through submitting to the Holy Spirit, who teaches believers the "mind of Christ" (v. 16).

The Corinthians failed to see the implications of this message for how they lived. They evidently believed in the gospel (1:2) but failed to live it out through changed attitudes and behavior. They thought they were spiritually mature, but they were actually "infants" (3:1), because they were acting like the world through their fleshly behavior (vv. 1-3). God's Spirit is at work revealing the new life in Christ, but people must respond to the

Spirit's leading. Paul visualizes a new world in his letter, where power and wisdom come through humble obedience to the way of the cross. The cross offers the possibility of transformation to the Corinthians.

The letter makes a major shift in chapters 5–11, which focus on how to live as holy and loving people in a hostile cultural environment full of immorality and idolatry. Paul guides the Corinthians in these chapters by setting up boundaries that determine proper behavior for believers in Jesus Christ. Many of the problems they faced were related to the influence of their pagan environment and a fundamental misunderstanding of Paul's message.

Chapters 5–7 mainly address issues of "sexual immorality" (*porneia*) and the importance of living pure lives as the people of God. Sexual immorality was a common issue across the Roman Empire and especially in Corinth. Paul begins chapter 5 by calling attention to a specific problem—that is, the church had not corrected a man in their midst who was having sexual relations with his father's wife. The key principle is found in verse 7: because Christ is our Passover Lamb and has been sacrificed for our sins, any sinful behavior must stop and be rejected by the church. After this, in 6:1-11, Paul addresses the issue of believers taking other believers to court. The key principle is found in verses 9-11: because we have been purified from sin, we should not be involved in sinful actions anymore. Verse 12 shifts back to the problem of sexual immorality, especially as it applies to prostitution. The rest of the chapter provides a good illustration of Paul's moral exhortation, especially as it relates to his theology.

Clarifying Misunderstandings (1 Cor. 6:12-13)

Paul begins in verses 12-13 with a series of quotations. The punctuation of these has been added in modern times and is a matter of interpretation, since it was not present in the original Greek. Most modern translations put the first clause of each statement in quotation marks to show it to be a slogan current among the Corinthians, and the final clause is interpreted as Paul's reaction against the slogan. Paul acts as a ventriloquist and puts words into the mouths of the Corinthians to capture their attention and involve them in the discussion.[1] The slogans may also represent misunderstandings of Paul's ethical teaching.

All three slogans are related and give expression to the same wrong thinking. The first slogan (v. 12) is a logical conclusion based on Paul's message of freedom in Christ (Rom. 8:1-2; Gal. 5:1, 13). The statement is repeated four times in 1 Corinthians (twice in 6:12 and twice in 10:23), implying that this was a thought widely accepted in the church. Because believers are "free in Christ" (see Rom. 8:2), it would not be too great a leap to conclude that "all things are lawful for me" (1 Cor. 6:12, ESV). Paul fought against a teaching in different churches described as antinomianism (no regard for the law). This may have been influenced by early Gnosticism, which taught that the spirit is good and the body evil. Some of the Corinthians may have believed they were filled with the Holy Spirit and so no longer needed to be concerned with matters of the physical body, including how they behaved.

Paul's answer to this is, "Not everything is beneficial" (v. 12). There is theological truth in the slogan, but the resulting behavior must be consistent with the new life in Christ—that is, it must be measured by holiness and love. One's behavior should benefit others and oneself by drawing everyone closer to Christ. It would be too easy to allow this slogan to become an excuse for fleshly living.

The second slogan is an exact repeat of the first but with a different answer: "I will not be controlled by anything" (v. 12, AT). The key word

---

1. Brian J. Dodd, "Paul's Paradigmatic 'I' and 1 Corinthians 6:12," *Journal for the Study of the New Testament* 59 (1995): 39-58.

exousiazō means "to have the right, freedom, authority, or control to do something." Although Christians are free in Christ from legalistically following the written law, they are bound to the even higher law of love that incorporates all of the written law (Rom. 13:9; Gal. 5:14). Christian freedom is limited by love. Because of their love for God and others, believers are not free to do whatever their fleshly lusts entice them to do (Rom. 13:10). Paul's later discussion on love in 1 Corinthians 13 is a crucial connection of his ethic with God's will for all people to love. Because the Corinthians were in danger of spiritual and moral bondage by being "controlled" (*exousiasthēsomai*, a passive verb) by the distorted desires of the flesh (6:12; see 3:1), the only lasting answer to this problem was the way of sanctified love empowered by the Holy Spirit.

The third slogan in 6:13 is more situationally specific: "Food is meant for the stomach and the stomach for food" (ESV). This statement reinforces the idea that the Corinthians misunderstood how believers should behave. They may have thought that since food does not matter, what happens to the body does not matter either; therefore, one is free to participate in any kind of sexual activity. Accordingly, Paul refutes the way this false thinking has given license to "sexual immorality" (*porneia*); he asserts that although the body and food are temporary to this world, both must be used for God's glory. Moreover, what happens with the body is directly related to one's relationship with God. If the Corinthians want to acknowledge the lordship of Christ, they must respond appropriately to Paul's exhortation.

Theological Indicative (1 Cor. 6:14-17)

In verse 14, Paul shifts to the theological foundation for his ethic. There is an allusion to bodily resurrection in this verse, a topic Paul takes up again in chapter 15. He includes this topic here because it provides a good illustration of the sacredness of the body: if the Lord's body could be raised, then there is nothing inherently evil about the human body. In fact, it, too, undergoes a transformation in Christ (Rom. 6:12-14; 8:9-11). There is no dichotomy between the body and spirit for Paul. Both can be completely sanctified (1 Thess. 5:23). In 1 Corinthians 6:14, Paul begins to connect the situation that needs correction in Corinth (ethical maxim) with his theological foundation in Christ.

Beginning in verse 15, Paul asks three rhetorical questions that move his logical argument further along. These questions share the same theme: being physically united with that which captures our heart. The phrase "do you not know" assumes that what Paul is saying is not new, or at least it should be self-evident to those who are growing in Christ, which the Corinthians were struggling to do. Our physical bodies are where we carry out God's purposes for us in Christ. Our holiness is not only spiritual but physical. Human flesh is not inherently sinful, although it can be used for selfish purposes to fulfill deceived and lustful desires. Paul develops this idea much more in Romans 6.

Finally, we are introduced to the specific problem of prostitution in the second rhetorical question in 1 Corinthians 6:15*b*. What has been sanctified to Christ and united with him through the Holy Spirit can "never" (the strong *mē genoito*; see Rom. 6:1-2) be united with a prostitute in the physical union of intercourse. The third rhetorical question makes this unity even more explicit, that intercourse unites two people physically; thus, prostitution unites two bodies together (1 Cor. 6:16). Paul adds further support by citing Genesis 2:24, that two people united in marriage become one flesh. He will show in 1 Corinthians 7 that sexual union is not wrong if done within holy marriage. But it is a contradiction to say that a believer can be united with a prostitute and united to Christ at the same time. The believer's body belongs to Christ because he or she has recognized Christ's supremacy.

Most English translations use a lowercase "s" for the word "spirit" (*pneuma*) in 6:17, interpreting it as a reference to the human spirit. The Greek does not include the article "the," so this is a reasonable interpretation. But in Paul's broader theology, it is the Holy Spirit who unites us with Christ. Although this unity begins within the human spirit, it incorporates one's whole being, including the physical body.

> **Much of the New Testament was written in response to the influence of pagan beliefs and practices upon the earliest Christians.**

Much of the New Testament was written in response to the influence of pagan beliefs and practices upon the earliest Christians. Sexual immorality and eating food sacrificed to idols, the two major issues Paul addresses in 1 Corinthians 5–10, were also the concerns of the council that met in Jerusalem to discuss the requirements of Gentile converts (see Acts 15). These two issues continued to plague the early church, as suggested by their mention again in reference to the churches in Pergamum and Thyatira in Revelation 2:14, 20. In 1 Thessalonians 4:3, Paul writes that it is God's will for us to be sanctified and to avoid sexual immorality.

Many of the problems in the Corinthian church were directly related to the syncretistic environment of the city of Corinth. The Christians in this church likely represented the different segments of the society, including Jews and Gentiles. Archaeological evidence shows the presence of numerous cults, temples, and shrines in the vicinity of Corinth. Like most ancient cities of the Roman Empire, first-century Corinth was full of immorality.

Some of the religious cults of the city glamorized sexual activity. The influential temple of Aphrodite was located on the rock called the

Acrocorinth, which rises in the middle of the Corinthian Isthmus. Worship of Aphrodite as the goddess of love and sexuality may have provided the inhabitants of Corinth an opportunity to participate in sensual enjoyment contrary to Paul's understanding of holiness. Present in the city was also the worship of Hera Argaea, the goddess of marriage and sexuality for women and of sacred marriage. The worship of Dionysus had a reputation for drunkenness and sexual immorality.[2] The Greeks typically saw nothing wrong with prostitution. They saw sexual intercourse just as natural, necessary, and justifiable as eating and drinking.[3]

Ethical Imperative (1 Cor. 6:18-20)

Verse 18 begins with the simple ethical imperative "flee sexual immorality" (*porneia*; NASB). This statement comes in the middle of all the reasons for following Paul's directive. In the previous verses, Paul has shown that Christian freedom is not a license to do whatever pleases the flesh (vv. 12-13). The body, as well as one's spirit, is to be sanctified as holy to the Lord. The body should be used for God's purposes and glory (v. 13). The body is part of God's plan and will someday be raised from the dead just as Christ's body was (v. 14). Our bodies are part of Christ through the Holy Spirit and should not be united to prostitutes (vv. 15-17). In the following verses, Paul will add further theological reasons why the Corinthians should avoid sexual immorality, especially prostitution.

The verb "flee" (*pheugete*) is in the imperative mood. This is the first use of this mood in this section. The root word can mean "to seek safety in flight," "to become safe from danger by eluding or avoiding it," and "to keep from doing something by avoiding it because of its potential

---

2. Wendell L. Willis, *Idol Meat in Corinth: The Pauline Argument in 1 Corinthians 8 and 10*, Society of Biblical Literature Dissertation Series 68 (Chico, CA: Scholars Press, 1985), 30.

3. Gerhard Kittel and Gerhard Friedrich, eds., *Theological Dictionary of the New Testament*, trans. Geoffrey W. Bromiley (Grand Rapids: Eerdmans, 1964-76), 4:582.

damage."[4] Paul uses the same word later in reference to idolatry (10:14). One of the further reasons to run away from sexual immorality is that it is a sin against one's own body. In Paul's reasoning here, sexuality immorality is the only sin that directly and uniquely affects one's own body. This should not be taken as an exclusive or exhaustive statement, but this does show how an outward act can significantly influence the inner person.

The next thought, in verse 19, provides an additional step in Paul's logic. He reasons that one's own body is actually not one's *own* but God's; it is the temple of the Holy Spirit. The word for "temple" (*naos*) refers to the sacred area of a deity's presence separated from the mundane and unholy around it. The use of temple imagery adds another theological basis for Paul's ethic. Most of the believers in Corinth, whether Gentile or Jewish, would have had psychological, emotional, or religious connections to temples. Paul may have had in mind the temple of Jerusalem.

In the Hebrew Scriptures, religious articles and priests underwent ritual sanctification to be fit for use in the temple (Exod. 25–31). The tabernacle, and later the temple, had to be pure and undefiled before God would allow his presence to dwell there (40:34; 1 Kings 9:3). What made the temple holy was God's presence. There was nothing intrinsically holy about the building, people, or objects that were part of the worship. Everything was holy relative to the divine presence. Although the temple was explicitly God's dwelling place in Israel, God also dwelled in the midst of the people themselves by his Holy Spirit (Isa. 63:9-14).

Paul used temple imagery earlier in the letter (1 Cor. 3:16-23) to encourage the Corinthians to keep their bodies holy and fit to be dwellings for the Holy Spirit. The assumption in chapter 6 is that by defiling their bodies with sexual immorality, they make themselves unworthy vessels for the Holy Spirit. The presence of the Holy Spirit is a matter of

---

4. Bauer et al., *Greek-English Lexicon*, 1052.

grace, represented in the phrase "whom you have received from God" (v. 19). This is the indicative of Paul's ethic.

Verses 19-20 give one of the clearest examples in Paul's letters of how he gives his moral exhortation. Both key elements are present: theological indicative and moral imperative. He uses two more indicative statements that emphasize God's grace. The thought of the two phrases is joined by a causal link. "You are not your own" because "you were bought at a price." The price is not stated, but Paul may have assumed that the Corinthians would realize the purchase price was Christ's death upon the cross (1:30). The Corinthians had been purchased off the slave block of sin and had been made holy and fit to be the temple of the Holy Spirit.

The second imperative broadens the first one in 6:18: the way to "flee sexual immorality" is to "glorify God in your body" (v. 20, NASB). Believers are only able to follow this command in the obedience of faith that responds to God's offer of forgiveness and cleansing in Christ. The logical conclusion to Paul's argument is straightforward: because of what God has done in Christ for us, any unholy behavior such as *porneia* cannot be accepted. Being united with Christ involves a break from the control of the flesh and distorted desires to satisfy one's selfishness and pride. Paul's goal is the holiness of both the community (3:16) and the individual (6:19).

Living as God's Holy Temples

With this clear understanding of the passage, we can explore its intended impact on how the Corinthians lived. Paul wants them to be an alternative to the types of temples so common in Corinth. They should not defile themselves as God's temple by participating in activities inconsistent with what it means to be new creations in Christ (2 Cor. 5:17). Paul's moral exhortation can be summed up in the admonition "Become who you are." The Holy Spirit had sanctified them through the sacrifice of

Christ (1 Cor. 1:30), but they needed to respond by rejecting any behavior inconsistent with this new life. The letter suggests that they may have been confused about this (3:1-3), so Paul writes to set clear boundaries between their pagan society and this new existence in Christ. These boundaries were determined by the cross of Jesus Christ (5:7).

Anthropology is a useful tool for interpreting texts that demand a change of behavior, such as 1 Corinthians 6:12-20. Paul creates a "map" of acceptable behavior for the Corinthians. That which is "pure" exists within the new boundary lines Paul creates. Jerome Neyrey writes, "In general, an object or action is pure (or clean, holy) when it conforms to the specific cultural norms that make up the symbolic system of a particular social group."[5] That which is pure is in its proper place; that which is polluted or considered "dirty" is out of place in the particular symbolic universe.

The Corinthians' worldview was different from Paul's, and this influenced their behavior. Their acceptance of sexual immorality showed that they were seeing things from a worldly and fleshly perspective. Paul challenged them to see things from the perspective of the crucified Christ and to allow the Holy Spirit to grow within them the "mind of Christ" (2:16).

Mary Douglas[6] provides an additional insight. The human body represents the social body on a small scale through boundaries (the body's defenses), structure (the relationship of body parts), and margins (entrance, exits, bodily exuviae). In order to control a group, one must control the bodies of the individuals in that group. By showing how the Corinthians could control their physical bodies, Paul was also determining the boundaries for the whole church. By keeping dirt out of the body on the individual level, and subsequently on the corporate level, the Corinthians would be able to keep themselves pure and establish distinct group boundaries. Paul makes clear what may have been a fuzzy boundary for them.

---

5. Jerome H. Neyrey, *Paul, in Other Words: A Cultural Reading of His Letters* (Louisville, KY: Westminster John Knox Press, 1990), 23.

6. Quoted in ibid., 105.

What the Corinthians did with their physical bodies revealed their true allegiance. Possibly Paul begins the body of this letter with a discussion of the cross (1:18) because the cross should be the primary determinant of behavior. It is through the cross that the Corinthians were purchased from their slavery to sin (6:20). They had to make a clear decision through the Holy Spirit to recognize the lordship of Jesus Christ (12:3).

By creating strong individual boundaries, Paul was also defining who was in the church and who was living according to the ways of the world. Sexual immorality polluted the human body and would work its way into the whole church like leaven in bread (5:6-8). By living as their pagan society did and reveling in prostitution, the Corinthians were revealing where their allegiance lay. Paul's rules helped define acceptable behavior for those who were *in Christ*. What happened on the individual level impacted what happened on the group level. Through his rhetoric, Paul shamed the Corinthians into changing their behavior. He clarified that they were outside of the acceptable boundaries for those who belong to Christ; they were not acting like the holy temple of God.

The Corinthians would not be able to change their behavior by their own power. The slogans in 6:12-13 show how their thinking was wrong. The only way they could change their behavior was through God's grace. But God's grace had come and was evident in the cross. They had experienced this grace. Now, they had to respond in obedience. Paul expects this obedience by using direct imperatives that leave no question about what they should or should not do.

From this reading and contextualization, it is not difficult to jump to the truths that apply to our own situations today. These verses are a call to become countercultural by following values that may be at odds in the larger society.[7] The boundaries are determined by living in ongoing

---

7. Ben Witherington III, *Conflict and Community in Corinth: A Socio-Rhetorical Commentary on 1 and 2 Corinthians* (Grand Rapids: Eerdmans, 1995), 155.

fellowship with the Holy Spirit, who will teach us the mind of Christ and how to live as people transformed through God's grace in Christ. Behavior that matches the immoral culture is outside of the boundaries of holiness and is shameful before God. It is inconsistent with being *in Christ*. Paul's equating the behavior of the Corinthians with that of the "outsiders" should have caused the Corinthians to feel ashamed. The brighter the exposure, the more evident the deviance will become.

This holy ethic is a sign of loyalty to Christ. Paul wants the Corinthian church to realize it had been washed clean from the corruptions of sin. He attempts to resocialize the Corinthians in the light of this new reality in Christ. Forming a new identity in Christ may create conflict with the accepted behaviors of the larger society.

Paul tries to create a new community based on an ethic of holiness and love by placing boundaries around the community and by enhancing fellowship within the community. This can be seen with his call to be distinct from the immoral and idolatrous world by his "insider" language. Fuzzy or inadequate theology will lead to unclear boundaries between the church and the world. Having a sense of shame before the world can be replaced by having assurance of one's status and spiritual freedom in Christ.

7

Vice and Virtue Lists

THE LETTER TO TITUS

Vice and virtue lists are a particular subgenre Paul uses in all of his letters except 1 and 2 Thessalonians and Philemon. He did not invent this literary form but borrowed it from the common thinking of his time. The Old Testament does not include vice and virtue lists as a subgenre. Proverbs provides many simple statements of vices and virtues, but not in list form. Jesus did not use this type of list; the closest he comes are the Beatitudes (Matt. 5:1-12). The Jewish wisdom tradition from the intertestamental period indicates that Jews began to create such lists (Wis. 14:25-26 is similar to Rom. 1:29-31). Jews attributed idolatry to be the root of many bad behaviors. This tradition may have been influenced by the vice and virtue lists that began to appear in Greek literature in the centuries before Christ, particularly among the Stoic philosophers.

Associating certain behaviors with wickedness or righteousness is common to all religions. Vice and virtue lists as a literary genre were a convenient way to provide ethical teaching in a summary fashion. Plato designated four "cardinal" virtues of courage, wisdom, prudence, and justice.[1] The use of lists grew during the Hellenistic period. Zeno (340–265 BC), the founder of Stoicism, developed ethical catalogs of virtues. Those who followed him continued this practice. Philo (20 BC–AD 50) included a list of 147 vices in his treatise on Cain and Abel.[2] The use of such lists was

---

1. Plato, *Republic of Plato*, secs. 426-35, trans. A. D. Lindsay, 126-39.
2. Philo, *De sacrificiis Abelis et Caini* [On the sacrifices of Cain and Abel], sec. 32. See Charles Duke Yonge, with Philo of Alexandria, *The Works of Philo: Complete and Unabridged* (Peabody, MA: Hendrickson, 1995), 98.

not dependent upon direct Hellenistic influence, as indicated in the Qumran scroll *Rule of the Community* (1QS 4:3-11), which gives a list of vices and virtues that fits its dualism between righteousness and wickedness.

Paul's lists show many similarities with other lists of the time. Almost every ethical norm in his letters can be found in the writings of the moral philosophers. The primary difference—and this is significant—with Paul's lists is theological. Christian moral behavior is always a response to God's grace in Christ, empowered by the Holy Spirit, anchored in love, resulting in holy actions. Bad behavior results from sin and must be forgiven and rejected in response to the Holy Spirit. Virtues should result through transformation as an expression of faith and love for Jesus Christ.

There are many different types of lists in the New Testament. These lists are usually easy to recognize as a distinct subgenre because of their moral focus and their appearance as a list. The number of items needed to make up a "list" is debated, but usually at least three are required. The grammar of the lists may include nouns, verbs, adjectives, or longer phrases. Sometimes there is alliteration, assonance, *inclusio*,[3] or some other literary feature evident in the Greek but occasionally lost in English translations.

There are over two dozen vice and virtue lists in Paul's letters. Kruse identifies five functions for these lists:

1. To depict the depravity of unbelievers (Rom. 1:29-31; 1 Cor. 5:9-11)

2. To encourage believers to avoid the vices and practice the virtues (Rom. 13:13; 2 Cor. 12:20; Gal. 5:19-23; Eph. 4:25-32; 5:3-5; Phil. 4:8-9; Col. 3:5, 8, 12)

3. To expose or denounce the failure of the false teachers (1 Tim. 1:9-10; 6:4-5)

---

3. *Inclusio* is a biblical text that begins and ends with the same or similar phrase or concept. See *Handbook of Biblical Criticism*, by Richard N. Soulen, 2nd ed. (Atlanta: John Knox Press, 1981), s.v. "*Inclusio*."

4. To describe what is required of church leaders (1 Tim. 3:2-7, 8-13; 6:11; 2 Tim. 2:22-25; Titus 1:6-8)

5. To advise a young pastor (2 Tim. 3:2-5)[4]

These lists function rhetorically in Paul's letters to show how Christians should or should not behave. These lists are not exhaustive but illustrative of this expected behavior. These lists are often given in the style of two forms of exhortation. *Protreptic* exhortation warns about the dangers of the old way of life before a person becomes a believer in Jesus Christ, and it calls the person to the new life in Christ. Unbelievers are called to leave behind the old ways and embrace the new life in Christ by crucifying the old self with its corrupted desires (Eph. 4:18-23). *Paraenetic* exhortation calls believers to continue living in the new way of life. Often there is little distinction between these two.[5]

These lists also help define social boundaries and the expected behavior of believers who become part of the new community of the church. On the one hand, behavior that matches the vices will bring shame before God and other believers and ruin Christian testimony before unbelievers. It must be avoided because it is the way of the world. On the other hand, following the virtues is the honorable course to take because this is what the Holy Spirit teaches and is consistent with the "mind of Christ." The lists assume that the readers will respond in the expected way and grow in holiness and love. For Paul, love is the highest virtue of all and the primary characteristic of those who are in Christ (Col. 3:14).

There are two strategies for interpreting vice and virtue lists. First, because these lists are focused on individual words or short phrases, they will require word studies. The meanings of words are determined by

---

4. C. G. Kruse, "Virtues and Vices," in *Dictionary of Paul and His Letters*, ed. Gerald F. Hawthorne, Ralph P. Martin, and Daniel G. Reid (Downers Grove, IL: InterVarsity Press, 1993), 962.

5. Stowers, *Letter Writing*, 92-93.

several factors. The *etymology* of a word examines the word's root meaning and history of usage. This helps determine the *semantic domain* or range of possible meanings of the word. There may be multiple possibilities at this point, especially when translating into a different language, so *context* can narrow the possibilities. Often with certain words it may be more strategic to consider a range of possibilities rather than focus on only one. Several tools are useful for this type of study: a concordance to search for where the word occurs, a lexicon for the basic definition, and a theological wordbook for a more expanded explanation.

Second, words have no meaning by themselves but must be interpreted within their contexts. Each list serves a rhetorical purpose within its literary context. Paul supports this purpose with theology and application to the social situation of the particular individuals, church, or churches. As interpreters, we must determine if these lists are universal for all believers or if they were intended for specific situations. The more we understand about the historical and social contexts of a particular letter, the better we can determine this. Much of human behavior is universal but still culturally conditioned to some degree. Paul's vice and virtue lists can apply to modern Christians after making the necessary translation into contemporary terms and connecting the ancient situations to analogous situations today.

Paul's letter to Titus contains three clear lists: 1:6-9; 2:2-10; and 3:1-3. Paul wrote this letter to address the threat of false teachers from the "circumcision group" (1:10) who had gone to the island of Crete, where he had sent Titus. Paul wrote to guide Titus, his "true child in a common faith" (v. 4, ESV), in finding qualified leaders in the church who knew the truth of the gospel (v. 5). The salutation of the letter hints at Paul's purpose. Titus must help the Cretan Christians have a clear understanding of the "knowledge of the truth," "godliness," the "hope of eternal life," and the eternal gospel revealed in Jesus Christ (vv. 1-3). Part of Paul's rhetorical strategy is to provide a list of qualifications for leaders and various people groups within the church. By doing this, he defines orthodoxy and provides clear group boundaries of expected behaviors.

1. Titus 1:6-9

In the first list, Paul sets out the qualifications for the "elders in every town" (1:5). This is similar to the qualifications for overseers and deacons in 1 Timothy 3:1-13. First, in Titus 1:6, an elder should be "blameless" or "irreproachable" (*anenklētos*). Paul uses this word in 1 Corinthians 1:8 and Colossians 1:22 to convey how a person can be guiltless before God because of what Christ has done. This spiritual change should carry over to social relationships, where persons should have such a good reputation that no one can say anything bad about them. They cannot be blamed for anything. Everything that follows in this list will show how this can be achieved.

Second, the elder should be a "husband of one wife" (Titus 1:6, ESV). Marital commitment should be evidence of the good character Paul describes in these verses. The elder should serve as a good example to others of what a Christian marriage should look like. In a context of easy divorce and multiple wives or mistresses, this type of commitment would be a strong testimony of Christian love and submission (Eph. 5:22-33).

Third, an elder should have believing children (Titus 1:6). The Greek *pista* is an adjective modifying "children" and can be translated as "believing" or "faithful." The New Testament context implies that this faithfulness is connected to faith in Jesus Christ; thus these children are believers. Faith is something that must be passed on to the next generation. Elders will display their leadership ability by raising children who are believers.

The fourth qualification includes two negatives. An elder cannot be accused of being "wild" (*asōtias*), which can mean having "reckless abandon, debauchery, dissipation, profligacy."[6] This is the type of wild living led by the prodigal son in Luke 15:13. Getting drunk with wine can lead to this type of wanton pleasure and pursuit of fleshly desires (Eph. 5:18). We should abandon this lifestyle when we become believers and are filled with the Spirit (1 Pet. 4:4). An elder should also not be "disobedient" (*anypotakta*; Titus 1:6). This word means "refusing submission to authority, undisciplined, disobedient, rebellious."[7] The false teachers in Crete showed this type of behavior (v. 10). Avoiding these behaviors will strengthen the blamelessness of the elders.

The list continues in verse 7 but now applies to the "overseer" (*episkopon*) group. Interpreters disagree over whether or not this is the same group as the "elders" in verses 5-6. The word "overseer" implies some type of supervision or leadership in the church, possibly a group that leads the leaders. This is the same word used for the leaders Timothy should appoint in Ephesus (1 Tim. 3:1). First, an overseer should function as the "manager" (*oikonomon*) of God's household. Overseers have been given authority by the owner of the house and are responsible for protecting and developing the property and family of the owner (Luke 12:42; 16:1, 3, 8; 1 Cor. 4:1-2). In this position, an overseer, just like an elder, should be "blameless" (*anenklēton*; Titus 1:7).

Paul shifts to listing five vices to be avoided to preserve the blameless testimony and leadership of the overseers. First, an overseer should not be "arrogant" (*authadē*) (ESV). This word is characterized by selfishness that leads to being stubborn and wanting one's own way. This type of behavior overlooks the needs of others and uses people as a means to a selfish end. Second, an overseer should not get easily angry (*orgilon*). The root of this

---

6. Bauer et al., *Greek-English Lexicon*, 148.
7. Ibid., 91.

word is commonly translated as "anger" in the New Testament. Although anger can be justified in some situations, the negative context here implies that it is unjustified and likely a habitual response. An impatient leader is difficult to be around. Self-control and an even temperament will help a leader's testimony and effectiveness before the church and community. Third, an overseer should not get addicted to alcoholic beverages (*paroinon*), which could lead to a loss of self-control and open the door to many of the other vices in this list. Fourth, an overseer should not be violent by acting like a "bully" (*plēktēn*) (NASB). A leader should not physically or verbally abuse people. Fifth, an overseer should not be "greedy for money"

> **Self-control and an even temperament will help a leader's testimony and effectiveness before the church and community.**

(*aischrokerdē*) (NASB). In 1 Timothy 5:17, Paul seems to indicate that the church should support leaders in some way, and this might include financial support, but leaders should never seek to become rich, because it will lead to temptation (6:6-10).

Titus 1:8 shifts back to describing the desired virtues of overseers. First, an overseer should be "hospitable" (*philoxenon*). This word literally means "loving strangers." Hospitality was an important virtue in the early church. Towner comments, "The practice of hospitality among Christians was often urgent, sacrificial and risky: urgent because Christians might be forced from homes or jobs with no one to turn to but fellow Christians; sacrificial because material goods were often in short supply; risky because to associate oneself with those who had been forced out meant to identify with their cause."[8]

---

8. Philip H. Towner, *1–2 Timothy and Titus*, The IVP New Testament Commentary Series (Downers Grove, IL: InterVarsity Press, 1994), 227.

Second, an overseer should also "love what is good" (*philagathon*, a compound of "love" and "good"). This is a broad and inclusive term and depends on what is considered "good." These leaders should focus on "whatever is true, . . . noble, . . . right, . . . pure, . . . lovely, . . . admirable, . . . excellent or praiseworthy" (Phil. 4:8).

Third, an overseer should be "self-controlled" (*sōphrona*; Titus 1:8). This word occurs six times in this letter (2:2, 4-6, 12), which suggests that it was a particular challenge for Cretan culture. Avoiding extremes and having careful consideration for responsible action[9] provides a foundation for many other virtues listed in this letter. It is often helpful to consult other translations in a study like this. In this case, this word has a wide range: "prudent" (NRSV), "sober-minded" (NKJV), "live wisely" (NLT), and "self-restrained" (TNT).

Fourth, an overseer should live a "righteous" (*dikaion*) life (NASB). This important biblical word has both a theological and moral sense. Theologically, it is used for the justification God provides through grace (see 3:5, 7). Morally, it describes obedience to God's laws, which is likely more of the emphasis here.

Fifth, an overseer should be "holy" (*hosion*). This religious term has the connotation of something that is pleasing to God because it is without fault, dedicated, and pure. God is holy (Rev. 15:4) and expects those in relationship with him to be holy also.

The last virtue is the call to be "disciplined" (*enkratē*; Titus 1:8). It refers to "having one's emotions, impulses, or desires under control."[10] This word is similar to the word for "self-control" in Galatians 5:23 (*enkrateia*). The Holy Spirit helps a person gain control of the passions and appetites that lead to many vices and sins.

---

9. Bauer et al., *Greek-English Lexicon*, 987.
10. Ibid., 274.

The qualifications for overseers continue in Titus 1:9, not as a list of single words, but as a participial phrase possibly used instrumentally to show how the overseers could deal with the false teachers: "by holding firmly to the faithful word according to the teaching [they had received]" (AT). This last requirement connects the character qualities listed earlier with the critical need in Crete. Paul's list has included personal integrity, family, moral behavior, relational aptitude, and knowledge of doctrine. These leaders must set an example for the rest of the church by how they live.

2. Titus 2:2-10

After dealing with the false teachers in Titus 1, Paul moves on in 2:1-10 to give instructions for how the Cretan Christians should live in accordance with "sound doctrine" (v. 1). He will further explain this doctrine in verses 11-14. Behavior should be based on faith in Jesus Christ and proper knowledge about this faith. The focus of this section is on how people should behave in their homes and the church, which likely met in houses. If the various groups would follow Paul's lists of vices and virtues, they would be better equipped to deal with the false teachers who were ruining entire households (1:11). The household was the basic unit of Greco-Roman society, and it had certain expectations for how each person should act. Going against these norms could result in shame and the breakdown of relationships.

The characteristics Paul lists here were shared by the moral philosophers of the time. There is nothing uniquely Christian about them.[11] The behaviors listed are not particular to any age-group or family unit (like Eph. 5:21–6:9; Col. 3:18–4:1; 1 Pet. 2:18–3:7) but applicable to all

---

11. David C. Verner, *The Household of God: The Social World of the Pastoral Epistles*, Society of Biblical Literature Dissertation Series 71 (Chico, CA: Scholars Press, 1983), 145.

believers. Paul reinforces traditional behavior that would lead to a better testimony to nonbelievers (Titus 2:5, 10).

The first group addressed in verse 2 consists of older men. The descriptions listed here are similar to those in 1 Timothy 3:1-7. "Temperate" (*nēphalious*) literally means "to be sober and not drunk." Figuratively, it refers to being clearheaded or self-controlled. Cretans were known for their excessive drinking, especially among older people.[12] Being "worthy of respect" (*semnous*) comes by living an honorable life. A reputation takes time to develop, and these older men must earn it through a lifetime of integrity. Their reputations should be blameless, like those of the elders and overseers (Titus 1:6-7). Being "self-controlled" (*sōphronas*) is a human response to God's grace (2:2). Self-discipline requires "avoidance of extremes and careful consideration for responsible action."[13] This comes through controlling one's passions through careful thinking and sensibility. The idea of controlling oneself is important in this passage, with the root word occurring in verses 2, 4-6, and 12.

Finally, elders should be spiritually healthy (or "sound") "in faith, in love, and in endurance" (v. 2). The root of the participle *hygiainontas* ("sound"; origin of Eng. "hygiene") in verse 2 is similar to the "sound doctrine" (*hygiainousē*) in verse 1. The Greek article is used with "faith," stressing the content of Christian faith described in verses 11-14.[14] "Love" is an action that builds stronger relationships with God and others. "Endurance" maintains the "faith" and "love" under pressure and temptation. Paul often lists "faith," "hope," and "love" together (1 Cor. 13:13; Col. 1:5; 1 Thess. 1:3; 5:8), but here, in Titus 2:2, he replaces "hope" with "endurance." Endurance is how we live out our hope (1 Thess. 1:3; 1 Tim. 6:11).

---

12. Jerome D. Quinn, *The Letter to Titus*, Anchor Bible (Garden City, NY: Doubleday, 1990), 130.

13. Bauer et al., *Greek-English Lexicon*, 987.

14. William D. Mounce, *Pastoral Epistles*, Word Biblical Commentary (Nashville: Thomas Nelson, 2000), 409.

In Titus 2:3, the next group consists of older women who should act in a similar way by having reverent behavior. The word "reverent" (*hieroprepeis*) is found only here in the Greek Bible and describes something that is holy and dedicated to God, an inward, spiritual commitment evident in outward holiness. The women's holiness should be evident by not being "slanderers" or "gossipers" (*diabolous*). This word shares the same root with "devil," the great deceiver. Slandering is telling lies or half-truths, causing harm to others. The construction of the sentence shows a close relationship between slandering and being "slaves to much wine" (ESV). Addiction to alcohol can overpower a person's clear thinking and ruin relationships. Origen wrote, "Sobriety is the mother of virtues, drunkenness the mother of vices."[15] The final virtue prepares for the next list in verse 4. Older women must be good teachers (*kalodidaskalous*) in prudent behavior (*sōphronizōsin* of v. 4 is related to "self-control" of v. 2) by training the younger women in the qualities listed in verse 4.

The qualities Paul lists for young women are focused particularly on the home and describe how the ideal wife and mother would have acted in that time. Their strong family commitment should be evident in how they love their husbands and children. This love is expressed with two compound words that begin with *philo*, the common word for love and devotion within a family. The other descriptions in verse 5 show how the women can do this. They, too, must be "self-controlled" (*sōphronas*; see v. 2). In the context of marriage and family, it signifies modesty, an important feminine quality in the Hellenistic world.[16] Controlling their passions and thinking will also help them to be "pure" (*hagnas*). This word can also be translated as "holy" and is used in reference to objects that have been set

---

15. Origen, *Homiliae in Leviticum* [Homilies on Leviticus], 7.4, quoted in Peter Gorday, ed., *Colossians, 1–2 Thessalonians, 1–2 Timothy, Titus, Philemon*, Ancient Christian Commentary on Scripture, New Testament 9 (Downers Grove, IL: InterVarsity Press, 2000), 295.

16. Raymond F. Collins, *1 and 2 Timothy and Titus: A Commentary*, The New Testament Library (Louisville, KY: Westminster John Knox Press, 2002), 342.

aside as belonging to God. There is a strong ethical sense with this word that implies pure behavior and innocence from defilement.

Young women should work at home. In that cultural context, women were expected to carry out their roles at home by taking care of their families. Stott comments, "If a woman accepts the vocation of marriage, and has a husband and children, she will love and not neglect them."[17] The next word has a wide range of meanings, including "useful," "beneficial," "good," and "of high standard" (*agathas*). Women should be of the highest quality in how they live and act, especially with their families. Finally, they should submit to their own husbands (see Eph. 5:21-23; Col. 3:18; 1 Pet. 3:1). Showing respect and honor would be a significant witness not only to their families but also to nonbelievers. The goal, in Titus 2:5, is to keep God's message from being "malign[ed]" (NIV), "discredited" (NRSV), "reviled" (ESV), or "dishonored" (NASB).

The similarities in the lists continue ("likewise," *hōsautōs*) in verse 6 as Paul urges young men also to be "self-controlled" (*sōphronein*). This is the only direct reference to this group, but Paul continues by listing virtues that Titus, possibly a young man himself, needs to model to other young men. Titus could be an example by doing "good works" (v. 7, ESV). Doing good is an important topic in this letter (1:16; 2:14; 3:1, 8).

Titus could also be an example by how he teaches the church. Paul already gave the topic for Titus's teaching in 2:1: "sound doctrine." Titus should "show integrity" (*aphthorian*; v. 7). This rare word literally means "without decay."[18] Such teaching is pure, sound, and uncorrupted.[19] He should also teach with "dignity" (*semnotēta*) (ESV). The root meaning of this word is "above what is ordinary and therefore worthy of special

---

17. John R. W. Stott, *The Message of 1 Timothy and Titus* (Downers Grove, IL: InterVarsity Press, 1996), 189.
18. Collins, *Timothy and Titus*, 344.
19. Bauer et al., *Greek-English Lexicon*, 156.

respect."[20] It has the nuance of seriousness. Titus needs to ensure that the church members understand his teaching by stressing the importance of it for them. Finally, he must use sound speech (v. 8). "Sound" shares the same root as "healthy" (*hygiē*; vv. 1-2). Titus's words must be such that they "cannot be condemned" (*akatagnōston*; v. 8). This rare word comes from the courtroom and "describes the innocence of a person who is acquitted of a crime of which he or she has been accused."[21] If Titus teaches in this way, it will shame the false teachers and give him a strong testimony in the community.

The final group with a list consists of slaves (vv. 9-10). This list is more grammatically complex, with two infinitives and three participles. Since slaves were common in most households, it is not surprising that some had become believers. As they experienced new spiritual freedom in Christ, they may have been tempted to express this freedom in ways that created tension in the household. Paul's advice here offers a way that their lives can be a testimony of "teaching about God our Savior" (v. 10*b*).

First, slaves should be "submissive" (*hypotassesthai*) (ESV) in everything. This is an attitude all Christians should have that will bring harmony and respect (Rom. 13:1; 1 Cor. 16:16; Eph. 5:21; Col. 3:18; Titus 3:1; 1 Pet. 2:13). Slaves may not be able to gain their physical freedom, but they can use their spiritual freedom in Christ to show love to their masters. Next, they can seek "to please" (*euarestous*; Titus 2:9). There is no object noted here, but "if a slave does what is pleasing to God, the slave will usually be pleasing to the master."[22] One way to do this is by "not . . . talk[ing] back" (*antilegontas*) or being verbally disrespectful, which could create many problems for slaves. Another way to honor their masters and build relationships is by "not . . . steal[ing]" (*nosphizomenous*; v. 10). This

---

20. Ibid., 919.
21. Collins, *Timothy and Titus*, 20.
22. Mounce, *Pastoral Epistles*, 415.

rare word is used also for Ananias and Sapphira in Acts 5:2-3. This type of stealing involves subtle skimming or pilfering from the top so that no one notices anything is missing. The final item is an inclusive virtue of "showing all good faith" (Titus 2:10, ESV). The participle *endeiknume-nous* indicates that their faith should be demonstrated and evident so that they make the message of Jesus "attractive" (*kosmōsin*; v. 10). This word means literally "to put in order" and figuratively "to have an attractive appearance through decoration"[23] (origin of Eng. "cosmetic"). Through their submissive and honest behavior, slaves can be strong witnesses of their faith in Christ.

3. Titus 3:1-3

Paul gives one final clear list of vices and virtues that is inclusive of everyone in the church. This list is sandwiched in between two significant theological statements in 2:11-14 and 3:4-7. Paul's theology is always practical, and his ethics are always grounded in theology (see ch. 6, "Moral Exhortation"). In this case, the Cretan Christians can witness to God's grace in Christ by how they live before unbelievers. Grammatically made up of four infinitive clauses and one participial phrase, the list consists of what Paul wants Titus to remind the believers to do.

First, they should "be submissive to rulers and authorities" (3:1, ESV). These words possess the connotation of civil leaders. One motive for this is so that Christians might live "peaceful and quiet lives" (1 Tim. 2:1-2). Second, their submission should be evident by obedience (*peitharchein*). If everyone obeyed the laws, society would operate better and there would be peace and justice. Christians could not obey all laws, such as those that compromised their faith in Christ. Paul believed most laws are good. God gives authority to governments to promote good and punish evil (Rom.

---

23. Bauer et al., *Greek-English Lexicon*, 560.

13:1, 4; 1 Pet. 2:13, 14). For this reason, Christians ought to be model citizens by respecting those in authority.

Third, they must be "ready for every good work" (Titus 3:1, ESV). *Hetoimous* can mean "prepared for a purpose." Whatever good God has prepared for them, they must be ready to do (2 Cor. 9:8; Col. 1:10; 1 Tim. 5:10; 2 Tim. 2:21; 3:17; Titus 1:16). Doing good works will be the result of God's grace in Christ working in them through obedience to the Holy Spirit (Titus 3:8).

The next four virtues especially focus on relationships with others, divided into two vices and two virtues. The first vice uses the strong word "blaspheme" (*blasphēmein*; v. 2). When this word is used in human relationships, it describes speaking in a disrespectful way that demeans, denigrates, or maligns.[24] Belittling people and not treating them with respect usually leads to hurt feelings and the loss of witness.

The next infinitive "to be" is used with two adjectives (also found in 1 Tim. 3:3). The Cretans are to be "peaceable" (*amachous*; Titus 3:2). This word describes someone easy to get along with, who is not argumentative or combative. The opposite of this is being quarrelsome. Quarreling accomplishes little but always causes problems and should be rejected by believers (2 Tim. 2:23-24; Titus 3:9). One way to avoid quarrels is to be "gentle" (*epieikeis*; Titus 3:2, ESV). A person acts this way by being "yielding, gentle, kind, courteous, tolerant," by "not insisting on every right of letter of law or custom."[25] This will require humility, flexibility, and accommodation in one's interactions with others.

The last virtue is given in an instrumental participial phrase that shows how to be peaceful and gentle: "by showing all courtesy" (v. 2, AT). "Courtesy" (*prautēta*) is "the quality of not being overly impressed by a

---

24. Ibid., 178.
25. Ibid., 371.

sense of one's self-importance."[26] Different translations attempt to capture its range of nuances: "courtesy" (ESV, NRSV), "meekness" (KJV), "consideration" (NASB), and "humility" (NKJV). The root meaning is used for taming wild animals so they are calm. Greek culture highly prized gentle friendliness in relationships.[27] This virtue comes from a heart of love through the working of the Holy Spirit (1 Cor. 4:21; Gal. 5:23). This was one of the character traits of Jesus (Matt. 21:5; 2 Cor. 10:1) and part of his kingdom ethic (Matt. 5:5). This courtesy is to be shown to everyone, no exceptions.

The final vice list in Titus 3:3 sets up a contrast between how Christians once lived and how the grace of God changes them (vv. 4-7). This list focuses on relationship with God, self, and others. First, the old life is described as "foolish" (*anoētoi*). The root of this word refers to the "mind" or thinking. Unbelievers are ignorant of the things of God because of their lack of faith and rejection and rebellion against God's self-evident revelation (Luke 24:25; Rom. 1:14; 18-31; Eph. 4:18-19). Second, they are "disobedient" (*apeitheis*) because they reject God's laws and follow their own doomed thinking (Luke 1:17; Acts 26:19; Rom. 1:30; 2 Tim. 3:2). Foolishness leads to disobedience.

The grammar shifts to two passive participles that result from foolishness and disobedience with a focus on the self (Titus 3:3). The passive voice suggests that unbelievers are victims who are being "deceived" (*planōmenoi*) and "enslaved" (*douleuontes*). Deception involves twisting the truth into a lie so that it looks attractive. Paul may have chosen this word in reflection of the deceitful false teachers who were causing problems in Crete (1:10). Minimally, unbelievers are deceived by Satan, who uses the flesh to pull them into slavery to sin (2 Cor. 4:4; 11:3; 1 Tim.

---

26. Ibid., 861.
27. Kittel and Friedrich, *Theological Dictionary*, 6:645-46.

4:1-2; 2 Tim. 2:26). The deceived unbelievers become enslaved to "passions and pleasures" (Titus 3:3). The word for "passions" (*epithymiais*) is morally neutral but usually has a negative connotation in the New Testament. "Pleasures" (*hēdonais*) are feelings or sensations that bring delight. God gives us passions and pleasures, but these become distorted because of sin to the point that they control us and are used to please distorted, selfish, fleshly desires (Rom. 1:24; 2 Tim. 3:4). God's grace helps us overcome these (Titus 2:12) and leads us to sanctify our desires to him so they lead to holiness and righteousness (Rom. 6:22; 13:14).

The last four vices indicate how relationships are broken with others (Titus 3:3). The first two focus on attitudes that characterize the daily habits of unbelievers, and the last two on the results of these attitudes. "Malice" (*kakia*) is a broad term that incorporates all kinds of evil, wickedness, and depravity that can show up in "a mean-spirited or vicious attitude or disposition, malice, ill-will, malignity."[28] Malice is paired with "envy" or "jealousy" (*phthonō*). Depraved thinking shows up in selfishness, resentment, and coveting (Rom. 1:29; Gal. 5:21; 1 Tim. 6:4). These vices result in hatred (Titus 3:3). Two different words are used for hatred. The first (*stygētoi*) is found only here in the New Testament and is the response others give someone who is despicable, detestable, or loathsome.[29] The second is the more common word for rejecting and despising others (*misountes*). The present participle used here suggests that the breakdown of relationships with other people starts with rejecting God.

> **God's grace helps us overcome distorted passions and pleasures and leads us to sanctify our desires to him so they lead to holiness and righteousness.**

---

28. Bauer et al., *Greek-English Lexicon*, 500.
29. Ibid., 949.

The Power of Grace to Change

Paul wrote this letter to help Titus guide the Christians in Crete on how to live so that they could be strong witnesses of God's salvation in Jesus Christ. False teachers had come to the island and were teaching salvation through circumcision and certain works, but they themselves failed to live this out (Titus 1:10-16). Paul makes clear here, as he does in other letters, that righteousness comes through God's grace and not human effort (Rom. 3:23-24; Eph. 2:8-9).

Although the vice and virtue lists address this problem by speaking to specific groups, beginning with the leaders, these lists apply to all of us in one way or another. The character qualities Paul calls for are universal, evidenced even in how these qualities were common in the moral exhortations of the period. Although we may not think of dividing the church into the groups that Paul does in Titus 2, the types of behaviors listed there and in other places in the letter are broad and inclusive and generally characterize the "good Christian."

The call in all the lists is to experience the change God's grace makes in us, enabling us "to say 'No' to ungodliness and worldly passions, and to live self-controlled, upright and godly lives in this present age" (v. 12). The good news is that because of God's mercy, we can change the path we are on and live a new life. This new life will impact our attitude, behavior, and relationships with God and others. This is not something we do to earn our salvation but comes as a response to God's grace working in us. If we try to live these virtues or reject these vices on our own, we are doomed for failure.

The only way any of this is possible is because this grace has come in a person. God's mercy and grace have been "poured out on us generously through Jesus Christ our Savior" (3:6). Christian ethics are the response of faith and obedience to this hope we have in Christ. The Holy Spirit is the one who washes us clean from our past vices and renews us through Christ to live this new justified life (vv. 5, 7). Those around us will take note of the difference in how we live, which is the strongest witness we can have. What Chrysostom wrote long ago still holds true for today: "For the Greeks judge not of doctrines by the doctrine itself, but they make the life and conduct the test of the doctrines."[30]

---

30. John Chrysostom, "Homily 4 on Titus," in *Homilies on Titus*, comment on Titus 2:10, New Advent, https://www .newadvent.org/fathers/23084.htm.

8

Critiquing Culture—Women in Early Church Ministry

1 TIMOTHY 2:11-15 AND 1 CORINTHIANS 14:34-35

Timeless or Time-Bound?

One of the more divisive issues among Christian groups today is the involvement of women in ministry leadership, such as pastoring a local congregation or serving as a priest. Those who oppose ordaining women often appeal to certain passages in Paul's letters for their support. This issue can be reduced to a matter of interpretation of the biblical text. Careful and consistent methodology is required to arrive at conclusions that are faithful to the original context while also honoring the Bible as God's inspired Word for us today.

Two passages in particular cause challenges. In 1 Timothy 2:11-15, Paul (the supposed author) tells women to learn quietly and submissively (v. 11). They are not allowed to teach or exercise authority over a man (v. 12). And then even more shocking to modern readers, he writes that "women will be saved through childbearing" (v. 15). The other difficult passage is 1 Corinthians 14:34-35, where Paul also tells women to be silent in the church and be submissive (v. 34). If they want to ask something, they should check with their husbands at home (v. 35). This chapter will focus more on the passage from 1 Timothy, with some reference to the Corinthian passage.

Paul does not specifically address the issue of ordaining women in these passages. Modern readers arrive at this conclusion by combining three ideas from these texts: the ability to learn, having authority over men, and teaching and speaking in the church. To speak of an *ordained* minister is anachronistic, since this was a later development in church history.

There are four important questions that lead to an informed and accurate interpretation. These questions should be used with any passage in the Bible but are especially critical for controversial passages like these.

First, what does the text say? Here, we need to determine as clearly as possible the meanings of the words of the passage and how the literary context influences these meanings. Second, what does the historical or cultural context imply? This question may narrow or limit the possible meanings of the words and apply them to a particular situation. Third, what does the Bible as a whole teach? This is known as the "analogy of faith" and will help determine if this passage is a timeless truth that must be followed as written or if it is meant for a specific situation only. Fourth, what is the message of this passage for our situation today? Answering this last question cannot be rushed. The gathered evidence must be weighed before jumping to conclusions.

Examining the situation that prompted a work of writing narrows the possible meanings of the words. The crucial issue with any passage of Scripture, but especially one subject to different interpretations, is whether the truths it communicates are meant for a specific time, culture, and situation or are applicable to any culture or analogous situation without further adjustment or contextualization. Simply put, are Paul's directions about women in his letters intended for specific situations or are they universal truths that apply to our situations today without any further adjustment? Always behind every descriptive and contextualized truth there is a timeless principle that guides it. Minimally, as interpreters, we must discover this timeless truth and obediently apply it to our own situations.

As a final caution, it is crucial to set aside any personal agenda, including attempting to prove one way or the other that Paul or, by extension, God allows or rejects women for ministry leadership. The temptation is simply to ignore the difficult passages and appeal to broad theological principles found in other texts such as Galatians 3:28. To be fair to Paul and the biblical text, we must come to difficult passages with open minds, willing to allow our own agendas to be critiqued. The goal in this chapter is not to solve the current debate by taking one position or another but to listen carefully to Paul as an inspired writer of Scripture.

Looking around the Letter

An initial step in the process of interpretation is to understand the reasons Paul wrote this letter to Timothy.[1] Timothy was one of the close companions of Paul whom Paul often commissioned to handle difficult situations. Paul had sent Timothy to Ephesus to help the church contend with false teachers who were caught up in "myths and endless genealogies" (1 Tim. 1:3-4). These people had a fundamental misunderstanding of the gospel. In response to this, Paul gives directions to Timothy in this letter about finding qualified leaders who would ensure that the truth was being taught (ch. 3).

In chapter 1, Paul directs Timothy to approach this situation of false teachers with "love, which comes from a pure heart and a good conscience and a sincere faith" (v. 5). He then offers himself as an example of God's grace (vv. 12-17). In chapter 2, he turns to the two ways that change can happen in the Ephesian church: prayer for everyone and faithfulness to

---

1. For arguments about authorship, see David A. Ackerman, *1 and 2 Timothy/Titus*, New Beacon Bible Commentary (Kansas City: Beacon Hill Press of Kansas City, 2016), 35-43.

the truth of the gospel found in Christ Jesus, the mediator between God and people (vv. 1-7). The common theme that holds verses 8-15 together is proper worship practices that will ensure the truth of the gospel is proclaimed. The first issue is the attitude of men when they pray. When they come before God by lifting their hands as a sign of supplication, they should not have any "anger or disputing" (v. 8), which would represent insincerity. Next, Paul directs the women to dress modestly, not in a way that detracts from the worship of God (vv. 9-10). Verses 11-15 continue the theme of how women should act in worship.

Chapter 3 begins a new section that instructs Timothy about the character qualities needed in those who serve in leadership in the church. Three groups are addressed in this section: overseers, deacons, and wives or women. It is unclear who these women in verse 11 are. They could be deaconesses (women ministers) or wives of the deacons. They appear to be a third group in the church "worthy of respect," whose influence could be positive by being "temperate and trustworthy in everything" or negative as "malicious talkers."

Observing the Details of the Passage

As with any biblical passage, it is important to work at the level of the language, since that is how meaning is conveyed to the reader. The words must be accurately translated and defined. Since the meanings of words are determined by their relationship to one another, examining the grammar and syntax helps narrow the options to be considered.

In 1 Timothy 2:11, Paul instructs how a woman should learn. The word "woman" (*gynē*) is singular, suggesting that this is a general principle to be followed. This word can also be translated as "wife" (3:2). The issues in the chapter, however, appear broader than simply those between a husband and wife, but that could be a possible application of "men" or "husbands" (*andras*) in verse 8 and "women" or "wives" (*gynaikas*) of verses 9-10. The verb is a positive command, "let a woman learn" (ESV). The only way to grow in the truth of the gospel is to learn about it. Teaching and learning were part of Jesus's command to make disciples (Matt. 28:20) and were critical in the growth of the early church. Everyone was to be taught, including women. Jesus taught both men and women as disciples. This principle is a nonnegotiable requirement for the church. The topic of the learning is not mentioned here but likely included the gospel and Christian ethics (Rom. 16:17; 1 Cor. 14:31; Eph. 4:20, 22; Phil. 4:9; Col. 1:7; 2 Tim. 3:14; Titus 3:14).

The learning should be done in two ways, given in two prepositional phrases. "In quietness" (1 Tim. 2:11) has a range of meanings, from absolute silence to a gentle, meek, and peaceful spirit (see 1 Thess. 4:11; 2 Thess. 3:12). This type of attitude is respectful and listens. Later, Paul warns some of the young widows about talking too much and being busybodies and gossips (1 Tim. 5:13). This type of behavior would have made it difficult for them to learn. As the saying goes, if their mouths are open, their ears are closed. The second phrase, "in full submission," shows an attitude that accepts the authority of the teacher and makes the learning process go smoother (2:11). All Christians should submit (Eph. 5:21), particularly to spiritual leaders (Heb. 13:17; James 4:7; 1 Pet. 5:5). The women needed to be trained in order to deal with the heretics in Ephesus, but they needed to be good students to make this a success.

First Timothy 2:12 is where the text becomes more difficult. The role of women changes from students to teachers. The verb is a negative statement, "I do not permit," which has the force of a command because Paul, who has apostolic authority, is saying it. This same verb is used in the difficult verse of 1 Corinthians 14:34. Is this Paul's opinion, as he gives in 7:10, 12? Is it intended only for this situation? Or is it a timeless truth for all churches? There are no qualifiers, such as "in all the churches" (11:16; 14:33-34) or "in every place" (1 Tim. 2:8). The verse itself gives no indication, so evidence from culture and other Scriptures may be the deciding factor.

Three parallel infinitives complete the meaning of the main verb, "I do not permit," with the first two negatives contrasting with the last positive. The first infinitive is "to teach" (*didaskein*). Teaching was honored by Jews and Greeks and important in the early church. The ability to teach accurately was one of the necessary qualities for leaders in the Ephesian church (1 Tim. 3:2; 4:11, 13, 16; 5:17; 6:2; 2 Tim. 2:24; 4:2). The leaders needed to know the gospel well in order to identify the heretical teaching circulating among the churches.

Why would Paul prohibit women from participating in this teaching ministry? Women worked as teachers alongside Paul and Timothy. For example, Priscilla helped her husband, Aquila, teach Apollos, who was "a learned man" (Acts 18:24). Notably, this teaching took place in Ephesus upon Paul's command (vv. 2-3, 18, 24-28). Paul elsewhere commands all believers to teach and admonish one another, and this likely included women (Rom. 15:14; 1 Cor. 1:5; 14:26; Eph. 5:19; Col. 1:28; 3:16).

The gender may not be the issue, but the qualifications of the teachers. Many women in Ephesus may have simply lacked the qualifications to teach. Jewish women in general were not allowed to study the Torah directly but learned Scripture from their husbands. Gentile women also had little opportunity for education. Christian women were not categorically prohibited from teaching, since women could teach their children and other women (Titus 2:3-5). Timothy was taught by his mother and grandmother (2 Tim. 1:5; 3:15). Without any formal training, most women in the Ephesian church would have been unqualified to teach the more educated men who were present. Although this point is unprovable in the context of this letter, it may be added to the proverbial scale as inferential evidence.

The second infinitive (*authentein*) in 1 Timothy 2:12 is difficult to translate because it occurs only here in the New Testament. It is not the usual word Paul uses for "authority." It can mean "to assume a stance of independent authority, give orders to, dictate."[2] It has the nuance of being responsible or in charge of something, and, by extension, taking matters into one's own hands or claiming sovereignty or authorship. Baldwin suggests the verb can mean (1) to rule or reign sovereignly, (2) to control or dominate, (3) to act independently or flout the authority over someone, or (4) to be primarily responsible for or instigate something. The second and third definition fit better in this context.[3]

The last infinitive simply instructs women to be in quietness. If they were quiet, then they could more easily learn the truth of the gospel. Basically, Paul wants the women to be quiet students and learn from the properly appointed leaders of the church. Those women who pushed their agendas and spoke out against the leaders or possibly their husbands made it difficult for everyone to learn true doctrine and only created opportunity for the false teachers.

Contextual clues suggest that some of the women (or perhaps "wives") were breaking cultural norms and assuming authority that belonged to the men. The word "man" or "husband" is unclear, but the close proximity to chapter 3 suggests that these men were the leaders because of their character qualities, one of which was the ability to teach (v. 2). If the women overstepped their position in the church as students, doctrinal integrity could be ruined. Being good students required them to be quiet

2. Bauer et al., *Greek-English Lexicon*, 150.

3. Henry Scott Baldwin, "An Important Word: *Authenteō* in 1 Timothy 2:12," in *Women in the Church: A Fresh Analysis of 1 Timothy 2.9-15*, ed. Andreas J. Köstenberger and Thomas R. Schreiner (Grand Rapids: Baker Books, 2005), 45, 51.

learners from those who knew the truth and had been appointed as the leaders. Although the letter does not explicitly say, the young women of 5:13 could have become targets for the "enemy" (v. 14) to take advantage. Again, this evidence is not definitive but suggests that Paul's direction here is for the specific situation and not a timeless truth.

First Timothy 2:13 is linked to verse 12 by an explanatory "for." The following verses appeal to the Genesis account of the creation (Gen. 2; 1 Tim. 2:13) and disobedience (Gen. 3; 1 Tim. 2:14) of Adam and Eve as further proof of how the Ephesian women should act. Verse 13 recalls the order of creation in Genesis 2:7-8, 21-22. Although Adam was formed first, it was Eve who was deceived by the serpent and first ate the fruit from the Tree of the Knowledge of Good and Evil. Paul does not seem to be arguing theologically about the origin of sin, as he does in Romans 5:12. In Romans, Adam serves as the antitype for Christ. The emphasis here is not on what Adam did but on what happened to Eve. She sinned because she was deceived, thus being declared a sinner.

There is a noticeable shift from "Eve" in 1 Timothy 2:13 to "the woman" in verse 14. "Woman" is the same word used in verses 9-10. It could simply be a reference to the "woman" (*gynē*) of Genesis 3:13 (Septuagint) or more of a broad principle that applies to the women in Ephesus. The word "deceive" (*apataō*) means "enticing to sin through trickery"[4] (Eph. 5:6; James 1:26). The word occurs in two forms in 1 Timothy 2:14. The basic form is used first for Adam. The second use, in reference to Eve, is a compound, intensified form (Rom. 7:11, 16, 18; 2 Cor. 11:3; 2 Thess. 2:3) and may be stylistic, "serving to set the woman and the man apart in the fall and to stress the priority of the woman's deception."[5] It is very dangerous to be deceived as Eve was because it may result in sin. The Greek

---

4. Kittel and Friedrich, *Theological Dictionary*, 1:384-85.

5. Philip H. Towner, *The Letters to Timothy and Titus*, The New International Commentary on the New Testament (Grand Rapids: Eerdmans, 2006), 229.

word *parabasis* refers to transgressing the boundary of God's laws (1 Tim. 2:14; Rom. 4:15). The verb "became" is in the perfect tense (1 Tim. 2:14), which suggests that Eve's transgression is still possible to any woman who might also be deceived.

These verses serve as a warning to the women about being deceived. If they do not listen carefully to qualified teachers, they could end up being deceived by the false teachers who had infiltrated the church. This adds further evidence that this is a localized issue related to the problems arising in the Ephesian church.

Verse 15 offers additional challenges and clarification to the preceding verses. The "but" (*de*) at the beginning of verse 15 connects Eve's situation with that of the Ephesian women. The subject of the verb is singular with no noun serving as the subject, but the implied subject is the "woman" of verse 14. The question is the identity of the subject of this verb. Does this verse refer to Eve, a generic woman in a principled statement, or the women in the Ephesian church? The subject of the next verb becomes plural, expanding the principle of the first part of the verse to be more inclusive of the women in Ephesus.

> **If they do not listen carefully to qualified teachers, they could end up being deceived by the false teachers who had infiltrated the church.**

The difficult theological issue of the first part of verse 15 is the idea that a woman will be saved through childbearing. "Childbearing" (*teknogonia*) is a compound word occurring only elsewhere in 5:14, where it refers to physically giving birth to a child. What type of salvation is this, and how does giving birth affect this salvation? There are multiple answers to these questions. Since the creation account is in Paul's mind, he could be thinking of Genesis 3:16, where God told Eve that she would experience great pain in childbirth. First Timothy 2:15 may offer the answer to this consequence of Eve's sin. However, this option does not seem to fit the context of learning within the church. Christian women have the hope of avoiding eternal judgment, although they must experience the pain of temporal judgment through pain in childbearing.

The false teachers may have taught the speculative doctrine that women's pain was a sign of God's judgment upon them, so Paul reminds them that their salvation is not dependent upon whether or not they experience this pain. It may be that Paul is encouraging the women to experience their greatest role in life as mothers. Their greatest place of influence is not teaching in the church but bearing children and raising them in the Lord. When women embrace God's role for them in bearing children, they can avoid many temptations and be better able to work out their salvation.

The false teachers in their extreme asceticism may have rejected marriage and childbirth (1 Tim. 3:4, 12; 4:3).[6] They may have had an over-realized eschatology that prohibited marriage and certain foods (4:1-5). If marriage was banned, then bearing children was probably also criticized. Some of the Ephesian women may have neglected their culturally accepted role in the family and been tempted to "elevate their religious functions to the neglect of the 'the drudgery' of home and family responsibilities."[7] When they accept their role in the family and church, they will be more assured of their salvation than they would be if they were busybodies and gossips.

The end of 2:15 shows how the women can live out their salvation. Childbearing is not the real issue in salvation, but fulfilling this conditional clause is: "if they continue in faith and love and holiness, with self-control" (ESV). They must believe in Jesus as expressed in the genuine gospel, live this out in love and holiness, and show self-control in all they do. All of these virtues are the results of the Holy Spirit's work (Gal. 5:22-23;

---

6. Mounce, *Pastoral Epistles*, 146.

7. Sharon H. Gritz, *Paul, Women Teachers, and the Mother Goddess at Ephesus: A Study of 1 Timothy 2:9-15 in Light of the Religious and Cultural Milieu of the First Century* (Lanham, MD: University Press of America, 1991), 144.

Eph. 4:22; 2 Thess. 2:13). The way the women can demonstrate they are saved is by modeling the gospel in their homes.

The key points of this passage begin to emerge through this close reading of the text. Paul is directing the Ephesian women in the appropriate ways to learn for their setting. Their demeanor of quiet submissiveness would enable them to listen to those who had been chosen and qualified as the leaders and teachers of the congregation. This letter was written particularly to contend with the false teachers who had infiltrated the church. The best defense these women could have against these teachers was to fulfill their roles in their families, raising children and leading loving and holy lives of dedicated faith and self-control. If these verses were intended for the "wives" (*gynaikes*), then their faithfulness in marriage and being mothers would testify to their salvation.

Consulting the Cultural Context

Since some of the conclusions reached in the above study are only tentative, looking outside the text and into the cultural context may add further clarification and insight. Paul's instruction to the Ephesian women is consistent with the cultural expectations of women at that time. The household (*oikos*) was the center of life. The typical household included a father, mother, and children. Larger homes might include slaves, various workers, and guests. Each person was expected to behave in certain ways to ensure the stability of the home.

Jewish culture was traditionally patriarchal, with the father being the recognized leader of the home. This male dominance carried over to other parts of society, but gifted women still could serve in important roles. The Old Testament records many women who served in various positions of political and spiritual leadership, including Miriam (Exod. 15:20; Mic. 6:4), Deborah (Judg. 4:4; 5:7), and the prophetess Huldah (2 Kings

22:14). Women also served at the entrance to the tabernacle (Exod. 38:8; 1 Sam. 2:22). By and large, the woman's place was primarily in the home (Prov. 31:10-31). The only place women could teach was at home to their children.

In Greco-Roman culture, women also lived under the authority of fathers and husbands. The father as the head of the household had absolute authority over his wife and children. Keeping within the roles of superior and subordinate allowed the house to function smoothly. Anything outside the norm could create conflict. An important part of this involved the behavior and dress of women (1 Cor. 11:5-10; Titus 2:4-5; 1 Pet. 3:2-4).

By the time of the first century, a sexual revolution, called "the new Roman woman," was spreading across the Roman Empire.[8] Before Christ, Roman women were expected to dress modestly. Around 44 BC, some changes in Roman law gave more economic and social freedoms to women. Some women began to dress differently, involve themselves in civic affairs, and lead sexually promiscuous lifestyles. These "new women" also were known for behaving loudly in public and interrupting speeches. By the middle of the first century when Paul wrote this letter, this egalitarian trend had reached eastern cities, such as Ephesus, especially among wealthier women.

Women could serve in certain cults as high priests. They experienced great freedom in the cult of Artemis, the great mother goddess, which had a large temple in Ephesus. If women received any education, it was equivalent to that of elementary school. Wealthy women had the freedom to go where they wanted and even to attend public social events. Poor women usually had no formal education, and their lives revolved around the home. Many were forced into slavery and prostitution.

---

8. Bruce W. Winter, *Roman Wives, Roman Widows: The Appearance of New Women and the Pauline Communities* (Grand Rapids: Eerdmans, 2003).

These new freedoms could have attracted women in the Ephesian church, or some of the women could have come out of this type of situation and brought their behaviors with them. If this was the case, then it could explain why Paul uses such strong language here and instructs women not to teach or have authority over men. Any woman exercising the new freedoms would have been acting outside of the expected cultural norms and displaying behavior that came with a bad reputation.

Is this an isolated situation? Answering this question may help us determine if this is a localized or timeless truth. Significantly, many women served in leadership positions in the early church. Although none of the twelve apostles were women, many women followed Jesus as disciples and had close contact with him and the Twelve. Mary the mother of Jesus and other women were among the 120 persons filled with the Holy Spirit on the day of Pentecost and empowered to witness in fulfillment of Joel 2:28 (Acts 1:7-8, 14-15; 2:1-4; 2:17-18). Leadership in the early church was determined by the movement and gifting of the Holy Spirit and not by gender. All believers are called to serve (Eph. 4:12). There are actually more women than men named as ministry leaders in the New Testament, and most of these appear in Paul's letters (see Rom. 16). The New Testament records the names of many women who labored alongside Paul and other men in the mission of the church (Phil. 4:2-3).

As far as teaching or preaching, there were prophetesses in the early church, such as the four daughters of Philip (Acts 21:9) and the women in Corinth (1 Cor. 11:5). Women such as Priscilla were teachers (Acts 18:24-26; Titus 2:3-5). Phoebe is called a "minister" (*diakonon*) in Romans 16:1 (AT). Women also were leaders of their households (Acts 12:12; 16:14-15; Col. 4:15). They had important ministries in the church (1 Tim. 5:9-10). Some had the special calling of apostles, such as Junia, in Romans 16:7. The extent of women's ability to teach is unclear, but the evidence shows that the involvement of women in ministry and in proclaiming the gospel was considerable in the early church.

The difficult passage of 1 Corinthians 14:34-35 offers further insight, since many similar issues surround it as well. There is a textual variant related to these verses, with some manuscripts including them after verse 40. It appears that these verses even caused some controversy among scribes. There is also the possibility that these were an early interpolation in the manuscript tradition.[9] Some of the same words and concepts found in 1 Timothy are used in these two Corinthian verses, including "women" or "wives" (*gynaikes*), "submission" (*hypotassesthōsan*), "men" or "husbands" (*andras*), remaining silent and not speaking, and the "law," which corresponds to the story of Adam and Eve. The word translated as "disgraceful" in the NIV (*aischron*) can mean "being socially or morally unacceptable, shameful."[10] Honorable or shameful behavior is determined by the expectations of a given group. In this case, Paul defines shame in a way that was opposite of what women in Corinth were doing. These women may have been seeking attention (honor) that made it difficult for the gospel to be prophetically proclaimed in the Corinthian church.

The central issue here is not teaching but being quiet in the church and submitting. The verb "be in submission" is passive, and no object is mentioned to whom women submit. The assumption is that they must submit to church leaders. The context of chapter 14 indicates that some of the Corinthians were speaking in tongues and causing tension in the church. Paul wants everything to be done in an orderly way so that unbelievers can clearly hear the gospel (vv. 23-26; 40). He is giving common sense directions to a troubled and divided church that thought it was spiritually

9. A. C. Thiselton, *The First Epistle to the Corinthians: A Commentary on the Greek Text* (Grand Rapids: Eerdmans, 2000), 1146-62.

10. Bauer et al., *Greek-English Lexicon*, 29.

mature but actually was living like the world (3:1-3). Boisterous women may have been part of the problem.

These brief observations strongly suggest that these verses deal specifically with the local issues in Corinth and are thus time-bound truths for that situation. This conclusion implies that at times Paul had to give strong directions to women who caused various problems in the churches. Worship, teaching, and learning needed to be done in an orderly way so that all who were present could listen and learn the gospel and respond by putting their full faith in Jesus Christ.

Conclusions and Application

First Timothy appears to be ad hoc, addressing issues critical to the theological integrity of the Ephesian church as it confronted the encroaching heretical teachers. To contend with these heresies, Paul sent Timothy to guide the church in choosing qualified leaders who knew the gospel and how to teach it. Teaching and learning were critical to ensuring that this church continued in its growth and mission. The behavior of certain women can only be surmised. The limited textual and cultural evidence suggests that loud women who spoke out of turn or assumed authority without being qualified only fed the situation and caused more problems.

Methodologically, reading these verses out of their historical and literary context will lead to a misunderstanding of Paul's intent. He attempts to give structure to this church in a way that will accomplish several goals. First, he wants the women to grow spiritually through their knowledge of the gospel, to "continue in faith, love and holiness with propriety" (1 Tim. 2:15). Second, through the first goal, the witness of the church will be preserved in a culture where women were typically subordinate to men, especially in the home. Third, women can find their identity and purpose in ways unique to them, especially through motherhood.

Based on the accumulated evidence, we must conclude that Paul is writing to a specific situation in the Ephesian church. We should never formulate timeless truths and doctrines on passages that suggest application to a specific situation. This leads to the important question, what are the timeless truths in this passage that can apply to women and even men today? The above three goals identified by Paul are a good place to begin.

First, teaching has always been a vital part of being the church. Teaching (in all its forms) is the primary way the gospel is learned and applied in people's lives. Those who teach should evidence a godly character, knowledge of the truth, and an ability to communicate that knowledge in appropriate ways. Sometimes those who are missing these qualities will need to be silenced so that doctrine is not compromised and the church can grow into Christlikeness.

Second, the witness of the church as it interacts with the culture must be authentic, relevant, and appropriate. Believers must live out their faith in ways that attract positive interest and not alienate people. Since we find ourselves in so many different types of social situations today, we must be willing to set aside our privileges and positions in order to reach all parts of our society. It is not a matter of personal freedom, knowledge, or liberation, but of love (1 Cor. 8:1-3). Paul's own testimony of his loving sacrifice of any personal agenda provides a useful backdrop for this point: "I have become all things to all people so that by all possible means I might save some" (9:22).

> **Believers must live out their faith in ways that attract positive interest and not alienate people.**

Third, we must work out our salvation in our unique journeys in this life. No two people will share the same path. Culture or family may dictate certain expectations, but the message of hope in Jesus Christ will transcend these. We work out our faith in the place God has put us. Our situation or culture may be different from someone else's. This should not be seen as a problem (even if it causes us personal suffering) but as an opportunity for God's grace in Christ to be experienced in transformative ways (2 Cor. 12:9).

To use this passage to silence all women in church is a misinterpretation of Paul's purpose. There are broad theological principles in Paul's letters that put the mission of the church on a higher level than cultural expectations, even the Jewish or Greco-Roman social structures we find recorded in the Bible. The gospel liberates those who put their full trust in Jesus Christ and find their identity in their relationship with him. Both men and women are needed in ministry to help the church fulfill its mission in the world. They become partners "in Christ" (Gal. 3:28) and are empowered by the Holy Spirit to speak forth the message of Christ (Acts 2:17-18). God calls both men and women to use their gifts to build up the church.

9

Eschatology
1 THESSALONIANS 4:13–5:11

The basic meaning of the word "eschatology" is the "study of the end." Christians usually use it in reference to the end times and Jesus's second coming. Paul's thinking is thoroughly eschatological. Many other topics of his theology are built upon his eschatology. The concept of Jesus's imminent return and all the events and ideas that surround it pervade Paul's letters.

As with other writings by Paul, the historical and literary contexts are important to consider in reading eschatological passages. Two key issues must be carefully approached: (1) What theological presuppositions are present in the text or assumed in the background of the text? and (2) What is the rhetorical purpose or intended outcome of the text? Every passage must be allowed to speak for itself, but at the same time, there are broader assumptions that guide the meaning of a passage. The temptation is to read too much into Paul's letters or use a verse or even single words to formulate charts of end-time events. We must remember that Paul always wrote as a pastor about the immediate situations of his readers.

Theological Presuppositions

Eschatology is not so much a literary genre as a type of theological thinking that occurs in various literary types. To determine if a text has eschatological themes, one must first define these themes. Paul believed his gospel came by direct revelation from God (Gal. 1:11-12). Yet much of what he wrote is similar to what other Jews of the time were thinking. In particular, his eschatology shows similarities with Jewish apocalypticism. The word "apocalyptic" comes directly from the Greek and means "revelation."

Jewish apocalyptic developed as a particular eschatology and was expressed in literature emerging after the prophecies of Daniel (chs. 7–12) and Zechariah (chs. 1–6, 9–14). *First Enoch, 4 Ezra,* and *2 Baruch* specifically exhibit similarities with Paul's thought. This literature shared the belief that God would dramatically intervene in history by ending evil, judging the wicked, rewarding the righteous, and bringing a new day for Israel. There are two ages: this present evil age, which will come to an end when God intervenes, and a new age marked by God's triumph (*4 Ezra* 7:50). Belief about the latter included a messiah, punishment of the wicked and reward for the righteous, and the restoration of Israel.

Paul adopted many of these thoughts but significantly reinterpreted them in the light of the gospel. Jesus's death and resurrection redefined Paul's apocalyptic approach to eschatology. Jesus came at just the right point in history to bring about God's redemptive plan (Gal. 4:4). Jesus's death and resurrection brought an end to the power of sin and death (1 Cor. 15:54-57), while also ending the dominion of this present evil age (1:20; 2:6-8; 3:18; 2 Cor. 4:4; Gal. 1:4; Eph. 5:16). The dawn of a new age began with the empty tomb and is experienced as "new creation" for those who are "in Christ" (2 Cor. 5:17).

This salvation was part of God's plan before creation and is the very purpose for which we have been created (Eph. 1:4-14). This eschatology also influences Paul's moral exhortation for how believers should live between the two points of Christ's first and second coming. We presently live in an overlap of tension between the present evil age and the new age that will acknowledge Jesus as Messiah and Lord (1 Cor. 10:11). We experience resurrection power now through victory over the power of sin (Rom. 6:5-7) but still face weak bodies, poor judgment, and suffering (8:10-11). We can find victory over the temptations and powers of sin, self, and the deceived flesh, and we can find hope in the midst of suffering, through the indwelling Holy Spirit, who transforms us into the image of Christ from one degree of glory to the next (2 Cor. 3:18). Paul calls his readers to live this transformed life now in preparation for the coming day of the Lord.

Rhetorical Purposes

These ideas were a critical part of the message Paul preached everywhere. Apparently, his eschatology could be easily misunderstood, as indicated by his correspondence with the Corinthians and Thessalonians. His eschatology was always expressed in ways that address specific concerns of the churches. Therefore, it is important to understand the context of each letter.

Paul's "thinking about the end" is particularly apparent in his correspondence with the Thessalonians. He and his travel companions Silas and Timothy started the church in Thessalonica around the summer of 49, on the second missionary journey, and stayed for at least three Sabbaths before being run out of town (Acts 17:1-10). This was long enough to establish a small and vibrant church (v. 4). At some point, Paul sent Timothy back to check on the church. When Timothy returned to Paul, he reported some of their questions and concerns, thus prompting Paul to write 1 Thessalonians, which is possibly the first letter we have in our canon written by him.

It is essential when interpreting any one of Paul's letters to read through the entire letter, preferably without stopping. In this reading, we discover that the Thessalonians grew quickly in their faith and became an example to other churches (1:2-10). One of the topics Paul introduced to the church in his initial preaching was "to wait for [God's] Son from heaven, whom he raised from the dead—Jesus, who rescues us from the coming wrath" (v. 10). In 2:1-12 Paul shares his own motives for going to the city to preach the gospel and his methods in doing so. He praises the Thessalonians for their firm and quick response to the truth of the gospel, even when it meant suffering (vv. 13-16). One of the key topics of the letter is restated in verse 19: the coming again of our Lord Jesus. When Jesus comes again, Paul will boast about the Thessalonians' acceptance of the gospel. Timothy's visit confirmed that they had not given into the temptation to forsake their faith but were standing strong in the midst of persecution (3:1-10). One of the reasons Paul writes this letter was to confirm their faith and encourage them to be blameless in holiness until Jesus comes again (vv. 11-13). In chapter 4, Paul gives clear guidance about certain troubling moral issues they faced, particularly the need to be sexually pure.

And then in 4:13–5:11, Paul addresses another major concern, possibly the primary reason he wrote the letter. The Thessalonians had heard enough of Paul's apocalyptic preaching while he was there to believe that Jesus would come again, but they became confused when some of their members died and Jesus had not yet returned. The eschatological themes introduced in this letter are expanded further in the second letter, particularly 2 Thessalonians 2:1-12. The same methodological approach used to interpret 1 Thessalonians 4:13–5:11 can be used with the second letter.

Concern for Those Who Have Died (1 Thess. 4:13-18)

With this background before us, we can now look at the details of the text. The paragraph of 4:13-18 can be divided into four thematic parts. Verse 13 introduces the key topic of this section. Verse 14 gives the theological foundation in the form of a creed that expresses Paul's message in simple terms. Verses 15-17 give a word from the Lord and provide insights into Paul's eschatology. Verse 18 ends with the application in the form of an exhortation.

Verse 13 introduces the next section in the letter with "but" (ESV), linking it with what came before. At first glance, it may appear that this is a whole new topic. But Paul's larger goal is application and helping the Thessalonians learn what it means to live as sanctified believers (v. 3). Eschatology for Paul is directly linked to life in the present (see v. 18). He does not want the Thessalonians to be ignorant of the topic he is about to discuss. That he wants them to pay close attention is stressed by the direct address "brothers" (ESV). The problem is that some people have fallen "asleep" (ESV). The context indicates that Paul is not referring to the sleep our bodies experience each night but is speaking euphemistically of those who have died (see Mark 5:39). Paul gives no further explanation of what this "sleep" is like, so interpreters should be careful not to form a theology of death based on this one reference.

The reason why Paul writes here is expressed in the form of a purpose clause ("so that" [Gk., *hina*]). The death of some in the church led to the church grieving over this loss. Grieving in this way is a sign of hopelessness; it is the reaction of those who believe this life is all there is (1 Cor. 15:18-19). Paul reminds the Thessalonians that they are not like these people. Such people, so it is assumed, are unbelievers, possibly those from 1 Thessalonians 4:5 "who do not know God." Paul wants to make sure that the Thessalonians have a different outlook—one that is characterized by hope. Hope is a crucial element in Paul's eschatology and is mentioned three other times in this letter (1:3; 2:19; 5:8).

In 4:14, Paul next gives the reason (the conjunction "for") why the Thessalonians should have this hope. This is the answer for those of verse

13 who have no hope. There are three essential affirmations for this hope introduced in the form of a creed marked by "we believe": Jesus died, rose from the dead, and will come again. Everything else rests upon this crucial confession of faith. "Through Jesus" shows the source of this hope (ESV). Christians are people of hope because of what Jesus has and will do. Significantly, God is the primary actor in this eschatological drama: "God will bring." The identity of "those who have fallen asleep" is assumed to be believers who have died, like those in the Thessalonian church. The identity of "him" (ESV) anticipates the "Lord" of verse 17, a reference to Jesus's second coming. It is difficult to know what the prepositional phrase "with him" means (v. 14, ESV). Verse 16 suggests that Paul is referring in verse 14 to those who will be raised first and will be led by Jesus at the second coming. From the perspective of the living, the dead will be coming with Jesus.

With verse 15, Paul begins to delve into the details of his eschatology with a more specific answer to the Thessalonians' question. His answer comes in the form of a declaration from the Lord. "A word from the Lord" implies some degree of authority (ESV). How Paul got this word is unknown, whether from the teachings of the historical Jesus, as recorded in Matthew 24,[1] or from a special revelation from the resurrected Christ, as mentioned in Galatians 1:12. Paul is functioning as a prophet to the Thessalonians, helping them to find an answer to their challenging question. "That" introduces the content of this special word (1 Thess. 4:15, ESV).

> **Paul is functioning as a prophet to the Thessalonians, helping them to find an answer to their challenging question.**

---

1. Ben Witherington III, *1 and 2 Thessalonians: A Socio-Rhetorical Commentary* (Grand Rapids: Eerdmans, 2006), 135.

Two groups are mentioned next. Those who are alive include "we." Is Paul including himself with the expectation that he will be alive when Jesus comes again? Or is he grouping all believers into this "we," with the future return of Jesus remaining undesignated? There is no way to know the answer, and as interpreters, we should be careful not to speculate about questions that have no clear answer from the passage. Paul lived with a sense of expectancy, but he also engaged in a worldwide evangelistic mission that was beyond his personal means to fulfill.

The other group consists of those who have already died, which would be the key concern of the Thessalonians: *What is the fate of those who have already died?* This statement should give them assurance and relief that whether we live or die, we will be with the Lord at his return. "Those who have died will not be left behind nor suffer a disadvantage in comparison with those alive at the time of the climactic coming of Christ."[2] Paul could have simply stated this, but instead, he gives additional information to ground the Thessalonians more in his eschatology.

The word "precede" implies a sequence or order, which is clarified further in verses 16-17: the dead will rise first, and then those who are alive will meet them and the Lord. Paul uses an important eschatological word in this verse for the "coming" of the Lord. The Greek *parousia* has entered the English language as a technical theological word and refers to the second coming of Jesus, but it simply means "presence." Paul uses it in an eschatological sense for Jesus's second coming only in the Thessalonian correspondence (1 Thess. 2:19; 3:13; 4:15; 5:23; 2 Thess. 2:1, 8-9) and 1 Corinthians 15:23.

Verse 16 gives more details about the *parousia* of Jesus. Paul uses terms and images from the Old Testament, Jewish apocalyptic literature, and common notions of the time, but he reinterprets all of these in the light of

---

2. Jacob W. Elias, *1 and 2 Thessalonians* (Scottdale, PA: Herald Press, 1995), 175.

Jesus. There are both audio and visual effects in Jesus's second coming, as well as a sequence of four events that will unfold: First, there is the visual arrival of Jesus descending from heaven. Daniel's vision prophesied the coming of "one like a son of man" on the clouds of heaven (Dan. 7:13). Jesus predicted his second coming to be a fulfillment of this prophecy (Matt. 26:64). His coming will bring the present age to a close (1 Cor. 15:23-28).

Second, Jesus's coming will be announced by a "loud command" (1 Thess. 4:16). It is unstated who gives this command. The third event is the sound of the "voice of an archangel" (ESV). This voice could be the one who gives the loud command, or these could be two separate events. The fourth event is the "sound of the trumpet of God" (ESV). Trumpets were used in the ancient world for announcements and to give directions on the battlefield. The blowing of a trumpet is connected with the day of the Lord in Isaiah 27:13, Joel 2:1, and Zechariah 9:14. The sounding of a trumpet at the resurrection was part of Paul's eschatological preaching, as 1 Corinthians 15:52-53 indicates. The assumption is that these three sounds will be loud enough for everyone to hear. It is possible that Paul is describing the Lord being escorted for the remainder of the journey to earth by his people—both those newly raised from the dead and those remaining alive.[3]

After these visual and audio events, "the dead in Christ will rise first." Two significant thoughts are given in this statement. First, these are believers who are *in Christ*. Second, the dead will rise to meet the Lord before the living. The challenge for interpreters is the expanse of time between death and resurrection. Are we with the Lord at death (i.e., we go straight to heaven), or will we join the Lord at his coming? Theologians debate this question, but it does not seem to be a concern for Paul.

---

3. F. F. Bruce, *1 and 2 Thessalonians*, Word Biblical Commentary (Waco, TX: Word Books, 1982), 103.

One of the useful rules of interpretation is to look for clues for questions like this in the same document or in writings by the same author, but this should not supersede the immediate context. Paul leaves a lot unstated in 1 Thessalonians, probably because he is mainly concerned about answering a question about the Thessalonian Christians who have died. He simply wants to give the living Thessalonians the assurance that all who believe in Christ will be with him in the resurrection. Those who have died are already in a sense "with the Lord" (2 Cor. 5:8). Based on what he writes in 1 Corinthians 15:52-54, the raising of the dead in Christ refers to a resurrection to a new immortal state of existence. In 2 Corinthians 5:2, Paul describes this as our "heavenly dwelling," or a body fit for heaven. The resurrection of the dead was a fundamental teaching of Paul (1 Cor. 15:13-18). The Jewish belief in resurrection goes back at least to Daniel 12:2. The Pharisees of the first century, of whom Paul was one, believed in resurrection (Acts 23:8). Whatever the state of the dead until that moment, their new existence will allow them to meet the Lord in the clouds (1 Thess. 4:17).

Verse 17 adds further insight into his eschatology. The identity of the "we who are alive" (ESV) would include the Thessalonians, Paul, and any believers who may happen to be alive when Jesus returns. These people are described as being left behind, still in this earthly existence. The major question of this verse comes with the word "caught up." The English word "rapture" comes from the Latin word in the Vulgate *rapio*, translated from the Greek *harpazō*. The Greek word means to "snatch away," as in forcefully stealing someone's property. Jesus's teaching in Matthew 24:40-41 describes two people working; one is taken and the other left. This is a strong deliverance from the evils of this present world. The idea of a secret rapture during the end times has been popularized in literature and in the theological perspective called dispensationalism. The basic interpretation is that believers will be raptured at some point in relation to a seven-year period of tribulation (pretribulation—the most popular, midtribulation, or posttribulation).

Again, we must determine what can and cannot be known based on what the text of the Bible clearly teaches. The idea of God gathering his people together is found in many places in the Old Testament, especially in reference to their return from exile (Isa. 11:12; 35:10; 40:11; 43:5; 60:4; Jer. 32:37; Ezek. 11:17; Zech. 10:10). A similar thought can be found in 2 Thessalonians 2:1 in another eschatological passage. Paul gives no specific details of this in relation to a period of tribulation. In 1 Thessalonians 4, as in 1 Corinthians 15, he writes simply and to the point and compresses Jesus's return into one great event of resurrection. To posit a "rapture" in relation to a seven-year tribulation requires a questionable reading and proof texting of certain passages in Daniel and Revelation.

For Paul in 1 Thessalonians 4, there is no time delay between a "rapture" and the coming of Jesus. Those alive in Christ will join with the dead in Christ for a meeting in the clouds (v. 17). The word "meeting" had a technical meaning in the Hellenistic world; it was used in reference to meeting and accompanying visiting dignitaries into cities.[4] Clouds were referenced in the Old Testament and apocalyptic literature for the presence of God, especially in theophanies (Exod. 19:16 25; Ps. 97:2).[5] This will be a special meeting because it will be a time of rejoicing when all believers will be with their Lord always from that point and forever more. It marks the completion of the divine plan of redemption and the end of this present evil age.

---

4. I. Howard Marshall, *1 and 2 Thessalonians*, The New Century Bible Commentary (Grand Rapids: Eerdmans, 1983), 131.

5. Ernest Best, *The First and Second Epistles to the Thessalonians*, Black's New Testament Commentary (London: Continuum, 1986), 198-99.

Paul intends this not to be an abstract prophetic dream in the unknown future. First Thessalonians 4:18 shows how his eschatology is always related to the present moment. He shifts to an imperative in this verse. The hope expressed in the passage should lead to encouraging one another. Those who were grieving the loss of their Christian brothers and sisters should not continue in their sorrow, because they know the final outcome for all believers: to "be with the Lord forever" (v. 17; Phil. 3:10-11). The coming of Jesus is not detached from everyday life. Encouraging others with this hope is something the whole church can do (as Paul intends with his use of the second person plural).

Being Ready for the Day of the Lord (5:1-11)

In the next section of the letter, Paul continues to apply his eschatology to the situation in Thessalonica. This section is introduced with "now about" (AT), a common phrase in Paul's letters for introducing a new topic of concern (4:9; 1 Cor. 7:1). The general theme is still Jesus's coming again, but now Paul is concerned about how the Thessalonians live while awaiting the new age in Christ to come in fullness. Paul may be addressing another question from them on the timing of the *parousia*. It is possible that they, like many today, had become preoccupied with trying to determine the time of Jesus's appearance and missed the crucial importance of how they ought to live while they wait. The assumption is that 1 Thessalonians 5:1-11 is about how those who are alive, as depicted in 4:13-18, should live until the day of Christ's return.

First Thessalonians 5:1 introduces the topic as the "times and dates." Two different Greek words are used in this phrase. They are usually differentiated as *chronos*, referring to a more open duration of time (short or long), and as *kairos*, referring to an opportunity at a specific moment in time. The use of both words here forms an idiomatic phrase echoing

Jesus's words that no one can know the time of his return (Acts 1:7; see Mark 13:32). This is a topic about which the Thessalonians should already know, possibly from the preaching of Paul or Timothy; however, they had missed the important ethical component.

In 1 Thessalonians 5:1-11 Paul uses mixed metaphors that depict two different ways of living, highlighted in the following chart:

the day of the lord	a thief in the night	(v. 2)
peace and safety	destruction . . . suddenly	(v. 3)
darkness	day	(v. 4)
children of the light	do not belong to the night	(v. 5)
children of the day	do not belong . . . to the darkness	(v. 5)
asleep	awake and sober	(v. 6)
sober	get drunk	(vv. 6-7, 7-8)
night	day	(vv. 7-8)
wrath	salvation	(v. 9)
awake	asleep	(v. 10)
died for us	live together with him	(v. 10).[6]

Verses 2-3 remind the Thessalonians of things they should have already known. Paul or someone else has evidently taught them about the coming day of the Lord. This "day" is mentioned many times in the Bible, with some variations in formulation. In Paul's letters, it refers to Jesus's second coming (1 Cor. 5:5; 2 Cor. 1:14; Phil. 1:6, 1:10; 2:16; 2 Thess. 2:2; 2 Tim. 1:12, 18; 4:8). He uses two different illustrations to remind them of *how* Jesus will come. As with any metaphor in the Bible, interpreters are challenged to find what part of the image the author is emphasizing. The first illustration of a thief in the night implies surprise. It is possible that Paul knew of the similar illustration by Jesus in relation to his second

---

6. Based on Elias, *Thessalonians*, 191.

coming in Matthew 24:43, where the emphasis is on being awake and ready for the thief at night.

The second illustration of a pregnant woman in labor stresses suddenness (*aiphnidios*; 1 Thess. 5:3). Jesus uses the illustration of pregnant women in his eschatological speech in Matthew 24:19, but with a different purpose than Paul here. The subject of the verb "saying" is unstated and implied in the third person plural verb (1 Thess. 5:3, NASB). The "whenever" (*hotan*; AT) at the beginning of the verse implies that this is a saying that people make often: "peace and security." People are comfortable thinking all is well and will always remain that way. But the surprise comes when death or destruction overtakes them. The expectant mother never knows when labor pains will set in. The last phrase preludes the wrath of judgment mentioned in verse 9. This is stressed by the double negative in Greek (*ou mē*): "They will never ever escape" (v. 3, AT). There will be no warning when Jesus comes again and no way to escape if we are not ready (Luke 21:34-36).

The passage shifts in 1 Thessalonian 5:4 with "but you" and applies the urgency of verses 2-3 to how the Thessalonians should live in the present. There is a sharp contrast between the generic "they" of verse 3 with the "you" of verse 4. Paul expands the idea of the nighttime, when thieves like to break in, and now compares darkness and light. These illustrations have a literal sense that quickly becomes metaphorical for Paul. What thieves do in stealing is characteristic of the nightlife. It is a time of drunkenness for evil people and sleep for those who think all is peaceful (see v. 7). The comparison of darkness and light is common in apocalyptic literature (such as in the Dead Sea *War Scroll* [1QM]) and the writings of John (John 1:3-5; 3:19; 8:12; 12:36; 1 John 1:5-7).

First Thessalonians 5:6 warns the Thessalonians against the laziness that comes with the nighttime (2 Cor. 6:14; Eph. 6:12). Paul includes

himself and other believers with the shift to the first person "we" and
the use of the command "let us" (1 Thess. 5:6). Being awake and sober
will avoid the dangers that happen at night, such as drunkenness, which
makes persons even more dulled to the events happening around them.
Being drunk or asleep symbolizes moral and spiritual laziness. Bad things
happen at night. Believers must be "awake and *sober*" (emphasis added),
which leads to *self-control* (the Gk. *nēphō* can be translated either way; 2
Tim. 4:5).

First Thessalonians 5:8 makes the contrast obvious and applies it
to the Thessalonians. Paul adds the metaphor of the protective gear of
the "breastplate of faith and love" and a "helmet, the hope of salvation"
(NASB). Faith, love, and hope are mentioned also in 1:3. These protect
the heart and the mind, the most important and vulnerable parts of the
body. The image of "putting on" has some possible connection to baptism
(Rom. 13:12-14; Gal. 3:27; Col. 3:9-10, 12-14) and could remind the
Thessalonians of the key resources they have as believers to fight the darkness. These three spiritual qualities should characterize believers who are
spiritually sober and prepared for Jesus's coming.

In 1 Thessalonians 5:9, "for" introduces the theological basis for these
ethics. Paul warns about God's wrath against those who are spiritually
drunk in the laziness of the night. God's purpose for humanity is not to
experience his wrath but to be given salvation through our Lord Jesus
Christ (Eph. 1:4-5). There is an implied choice behind this statement.
Judgment comes upon those who choose to live in the darkness. In particular, the Thessalonians should know better because they have been given
the light of the gospel. God's wrath awaits those who are found in the
darkness when Jesus comes on the clouds. The way to escape God's wrath
is through trusting in the atonement of Jesus's death. A key Pauline doctrine lies behind these verses: Jesus's death and resurrection assure victory

for all who believe in him (Rom. 5:6, 8; Gal. 1:3-4; 2:20). It is never too late to wake up from the darkness of night. In 1 Thessalonians 5:10, Paul connects these ideas to 4:13-18 with the word "sleep." The verse can be paraphrased, "Christ died for us so that we can live with him, whether we are alive or dead when he comes again." The resurrected life begins in this lifetime (Rom. 6:4) and cannot be stopped by physical death.

This section in 1 Thessalonians 5 ends with a final exhortation like 4:18. There are two commands: "Encourage one another and build one another up" (5:11, ESV). The Thessalonians have been doing this but need to do so more because the day of the Lord is drawing closer. We never know when death will call or Jesus will come. Paul has given the Thessalonians just the information they need to live out this readiness with faith, love, and hope. This is not an individual activity but something the whole church should take up.

Significantly, Paul's eschatology in these two chapters is sandwiched in between calls to holiness. In 3:13, Paul prays that God will strengthen the hearts of the Thessalonians so they "will be blameless and holy in the presence of our God and Father when our Lord Jesus comes with all his holy ones." This is not a wishful prayer but a real possibility. Later, in 5:23-24, Paul makes this explicit: "May God himself, the God of peace, sanctify you through and through. May your whole spirit, soul and body be kept blameless at the coming of our Lord Jesus Christ. The one who calls you is faithful, and he will do it." God's will for the Thessalonians is that they live out this sanctification in tangible ways that set them apart as his people (4:3).

> **Paul has given the Thessalonians just the information they need to live out this readiness with faith, love, and hope.**

As interpreters, we must realize that some things can be known about Paul's view of the end, but many questions cannot be answered. We should not go hunting for hidden evidence to fill in a missing part of our end-time chart. Although we may be curious or confused about ideas related to the "last days," Paul's words to the Thessalonians help us focus on what is most important.

Paul's theology always leads to behavior change. Paul is not so concerned about details but about being ready. His letters should not be read as road maps of the end but as calls to live as faithful followers of Christ. Looking to the future should not distract us from holy living in the present. In Acts 1:7-8, Jesus warned his disciples about being caught up with questions about the days and times of his return. Rather, they should be engaged in the mission of making disciples. Although Paul was not present when Jesus said this, he still lived with a strong sense of fulfilling the mission to which Jesus had called him. As Paul reminds the Thessalonians in 1 Thessalonians 5:24, God has given us all we need to live out our sanctification until we either die or Jesus comes again.

Conclusion
WRITING FOR ETERNITY

Paul did a remarkable job of putting eternal words into brief letters to deal with pressing problems in the early church. We have to conclude that he had the divine help of the Holy Spirit breathing these ideas into his mind in such a way that these words still have power for us today. His letters are not simply historical but God's word to us today.

Yet what Paul did by translating the heavenly into the earthly is what ministers do today at least weekly. How well they do this will influence the vitality of the church. As Ephesians 4:11-13 says, "So Christ himself gave the apostles, the prophets, the evangelists, the pastors and teachers, to equip his people for works of service, so that the body of Christ may be built up until we all reach unity in the faith and in the knowledge of the Son of God and become mature, attaining to the whole measure of the fullness of Christ." How can this equipping happen unless someone speaks forth the good news in relevant and transforming ways?

Preachers of today are not stuck out there on their own to think of creative words to say that will somehow bring change in the lives of people. There has to be a fundamental difference between the politician, newscaster, inspirational speaker, rabbi, or any other guru of communication, and those who proclaim the good news of Jesus Christ. The temptation that preachers face is allowing their own ideas to supersede those found in Scripture. The closer these ideas are to the ideas of the authors of Scripture, the more authority a preacher's words will have.

This is not only a challenge for preachers but even more basic for all believers. Paul challenged the Corinthians to grow up in their thinking. He writes in 1 Corinthians 3:2, "I gave you milk, not solid food, for you were not yet ready for it. Indeed, you are still not ready." To carry this illustration further, it is easy to dilute milk or add something to it to make it palatable, but solid food must be cut and chewed for a while. It takes effort to get a deeper understanding of the Bible. Paul's letters are not easy to cut and chew. There are parts that are soft and easy to eat like ice cream—parts that even a child can understand, but there are other parts that will take the sharpest steak knife in the cupboard to cut through. Using the sharpest knife we can find will be worth the effort. The more precise our interpretation, the better equipped we will be to understand and thus apply what we read in these letters.

One of the most vital tools to have in our box of resources is humility. We have to realize that the interpretive questions are not always easy to ask and sometimes cannot even be answered. Rather than get caught up in debates over miniscule interpretive issues that really have no answer, we can use our growing skills and understanding to catch hold of Paul's heart. Perhaps there is no simpler statement from his letters than Philippians 1:21: "For me, to live is Christ and to die is gain." When we read these letters, are we seeking to know the Messiah deeply? Are we allowing the Holy Spirit to teach us the "mind of Christ"? Are we opening ourselves in full surrender to the Spirit's transforming power in Christlikeness? As we delve further into the heart of Paul, we will find that he had a deep insight into God's will for living the sanctified life. May we come to better grasp and more fully appreciate Paul's understanding of this life—a life filled with love and powered by hope and faith.

Bibliography

Achtemeier, Paul J. *Romans*. Interpretation: A Bible Commentary for Teaching and Preaching. Atlanta: John Knox Press, 1985.

Ackerman, David A. *1 and 2 Timothy/Titus*. New Beacon Bible Commentary. Kansas City: Beacon Hill Press of Kansas City, 2016.

———. *Transformation in Christ: Paul's Experience of the Divine Mystery*. Eugene, OR: Wipf and Stock, 2019.

Aristotle. *Aristotle's Treatise on Rhetoric*. Translated by Theodore Buckley. London: Henry G. Bohn, 1850. https://archive.org/details/aristotlestreat00aris/page/10/mode/2up.

Aune, David E. *The New Testament in Its Literary Environment*. Philadelphia: Westminster Press, 1987.

Bahr, Gordon J. "Subscriptions in the Pauline Letters." *Journal of Biblical Literature* 87, no. 1 (1968): 27-41.

Baldwin, Henry Scott. "An Important Word: *Authenteō* in 1 Timothy 2:12." Pages 39-52 in *Women in the Church: A Fresh Analysis of 1 Timothy 2.9-15*. Edited by Andreas J. Köstenberger and Thomas R. Schreiner. Grand Rapids: Baker Books, 2005.

Barrett, C. K. "The Interpretation of the Old Testament in the New." In *From the Beginnings to Jerome*, ed. P. R. Ackroyd and C. F. Evans, 377-411. Vol. 1 of *The Cambridge History of the Bible*. Cambridge, UK: Cambridge University Press, 1970.

Bauer, Walter, Frederick W. Danker, W. F. Arndt, and F. Wilbur Gingrich. *A Greek-English Lexicon of the New Testament and Other Early Christian Literature*. 3rd ed. Chicago: University of Chicago Press, 2000.

Beker, Johan Christiann. *Paul the Apostle: The Triumph of God in Life and Thought*. Philadelphia: Fortress Press, 1980.

Best, Ernest. *The First and Second Epistles to the Thessalonians*. Black's New Testament Commentary. London: Continuum, 1986.

Bruce, F. F. *1 and 2 Thessalonians*. Word Biblical Commentary. Waco, TX: Word Books, 1982.

Campbell, W. S. "Old Testament in Paul." In *Dictionary of Paul and His Letters*, ed. Gerald F. Hawthorne, Ralph P. Martin, and Daniel G. Reid, 630-44. Downers Grove, IL: InterVarsity Press, 1993.

Chow, John K. *Patronage and Power: A Study of Social Networks in Corinth*. Journal for the Study of the New Testament Supplement Series 75. Sheffield, UK: JSOT Press, 1992.

Collins, Raymond F. *1 and 2 Timothy and Titus: A Commentary*. The New Testament Library. Louisville, KY: Westminster John Knox Press, 2002.

Deissmann, G. Adolf. *Bible Studies*. Translated by Alexander Grieve. Edinburgh: T. and T. Clark, 1901.

———. *Light from the Ancient East: The New Testament Illustrated by Recently Discovered Texts of the Graeco-Roman World*. Translated by Lionel R. M. Strachan. 4th ed. London: Hodder and Stoughton, 1927.

Demetrius. *Demetrius on Style: The Greek Text of Demetrius De Elocutione*. Translated by W. Rhys Roberts. Cambridge, UK: University Press, 1902. https://www.google.com/books/edition /Demetrius_On_Style/gjEMAQAAIAAJ?hl=en&gbpv=1&dq.

Dodd, Brian J. "Paul's Paradigmatic 'I' and 1 Corinthians 6:12." *Journal for the Study of the New Testament* 59 (1995): 39-58.

Doty, W. G. *Letters in Primitive Christianity*. Philadelphia: Fortress Press, 1973.

Douglas, Mary. *Natural Symbols: Explorations in Cosmology*. New York: Pantheon Books, 1982.

Dunn, James D. G. *Romans 9–16*. Word Biblical Commentary. Dallas: Word Books, 2002.

Elias, Jacob W. *1 and 2 Thessalonians*. Scottdale, PA: Herald Press, 1995.

Elliott, John H. *A Home for the Homeless: A Social-Scientific Criticism of 1 Peter, Its Situation and Strategy*. Minneapolis: Fortress Press, 1990.

———. *What Is Social-Scientific Criticism?* Minneapolis: Fortress Press, 1993.

Flemming, Dean. "Essence and Adaptation: Contextualization and the Heart of Paul's Gospel." PhD diss., University of Aberdeen, 1987.

Funk, Robert Walter. "The Apostolic *Parousia*: Form and Significance." In *Christian History and Interpretation: Studies Presented to John Knox*, ed. W. R. Farmer, C. F. D. Moule, and R. R. Niebuhr, 249-68. Cambridge, UK: Cambridge University Press, 1967.

Gorday, Peter, ed. *Colossians, 1–2 Thessalonians, 1–2 Timothy, Titus, Philemon*. Ancient Christian Commentary on Scripture, New Testament 9. Downers Grove, IL: InterVarsity Press, 2000.

Gray, Patrick. *Opening Paul's Letters: A Reader's Guide to Genre and Interpretation*. Grand Rapids: Baker, 2012.

Greathouse, William M., with George Lyons. *Romans 1–8*. New Beacon Bible Commentary. Kansas City: Beacon Hill Press of Kansas City, 2008.

———. *Romans 9–16*. New Beacon Bible Commentary. Kansas City: Beacon Hill Press of Kansas City, 2008.

Green, Joel B. *Seized by Truth: Reading the Bible as Scripture*. Nashville: Abingdon Press, 2007.

Gritz, Sharon H. *Paul, Women Teachers, and the Mother Goddess at Ephesus: A Study of 1 Timothy 2:9-15 in Light of the Religious and Cultural Milieu of the First Century*. Lanham, MD: University Press of America, 1991.

Hauck, Friedrich, and Seigfried Schulz. *pornē*. Pages 579-95 in vol. 6 of *Theological Dictionary of the New Testament*. Edited by Gerhard Kittel and Gerhard Friedrich. Translated by Geoffrey W. Bromiley. Grand Rapids: Eerdmans, 1968.

Hawthorne, Gerald F., Ralph P. Martin, and Daniel G. Reid. *Dictionary of Paul and His Letters*. Downers Grove, IL: InterVarsity Press, 1993.

Hays, Richard B. *Echoes of Scripture in the Letters of Paul*. New Haven, CT: Yale University Press, 1989.

Hays, Richard B., and Joel B. Green. "The Use of the Old Testament by New Testament Writers." In *Hearing the New Testament: Strategies for Interpretation*, ed. Joel B. Green, 222-38. Grand Rapids: Eerdmans, 1995.

Holmberg, Bengt. *Paul and Power: The Structure of Authority in the Primitive Church as Reflected in the Pauline Epistles*. Philadelphia: Fortress Press, 1980.

Ignatius, *To the Ephesians*. Pages 86-93 in *The Apostolic Fathers*. Translated by J. B. Lightfoot and J. R. Harmer. Edited by Michael W. Holmes. 2nd ed. Grand Rapids: Baker Book House, 1989.

Jewett, Robert. *Romans: A Commentary*. Hermeneia. Minneapolis: Fortress Press, 2007.

Kittel, Gerhard, and Gerhard Friedrich, eds. *Theological Dictionary of the New Testament*. Translated by Geoffrey W. Bromiley. 10 vols. Grand Rapids: Eerdmans, 1964-76.

Kruse, C. G. "Virtues and Vices." In *Dictionary of Paul and His Letters*, ed. Gerald F. Hawthorne, Ralph P. Martin, and Daniel G. Reid, 962-63. Downers Grove, IL: InterVarsity Press, 1993.

Bibliography

The Letter of the Romans to the Corinthians (1 Clement). Pages 28-64 in *The Apostolic Fathers.* Translated by J. B. Lightfoot and J. R. Harmer. Edited by Michael W. Holmes. 2nd ed. Grand Rapids: Baker Book House, 1989.

Lincoln, Andrew T. *Ephesians.* Word Biblical Commentary 42. Dallas: Word Books, 1990.

Longenecker, R. N. "Prolegomena to Paul's Use of Scripture in Romans." *Bulletin for Biblical Research* 7 (1997): 145-68.

Lyons, George, Robert W. Smith, and Kara Lyons-Pardue. *Ephesians/Colossians/Philemon.* New Beacon Bible Commentary. Kansas City: Beacon Hill Press of Kansas City, 2019.

Mack, Burton L. *Rhetoric and the New Testament.* Minneapolis: Fortress Press, 1990.

Malherbe, Abraham J. *Moral Exhortation: A Greco-Roman Sourcebook.* Philadelphia: Westminster Press, 1986.

Malina, Bruce J. *The New Testament World: Insights from Cultural Anthropology.* 3rd ed. Louisville, KY: Westminster John Knox Press, 2001.

———. "Religion in the World of Paul." *Biblical Theology Bulletin* 16 (1986): 92-101.

Marshall, I. Howard. *1 and 2 Thessalonians.* The New Century Bible Commentary. Grand Rapids: Eerdmans, 1983.

Metzger, Bruce M. *The Canon of the New Testament: Its Origin, Development, and Significance.* Oxford, UK: Oxford University Press, 1987.

Moo, Douglas J. *The Epistle to the Romans.* The New International Commentary on the New Testament. Grand Rapids: Eerdmans, 1996.

Mounce, William D. *Pastoral Epistles.* Word Biblical Commentary. Nashville: Thomas Nelson, 2000.

Murphy-O'Connor, Jerome. *Paul the Letter-Writer: His World, His Options, His Skills.* Collegeville, MN: Liturgical Press, 1995.

Neyrey, Jerome H. *Paul, in Other Words: A Cultural Reading of His Letters.* Louisville, KY: Westminster John Knox Press, 1990.

O'Brien, Peter T. *Introductory Thanksgivings in the Letters of Paul.* Leiden, NL: E. J. Brill, 1977.

Perelman, Chaïm, and L. Olbrechts-Tyteca. *The New Rhetoric: A Treatise on Argumentation.* Notre Dame, IN: University of Notre Dame, 1969.

Plato. *Plato's Phaedo.* Translated by F. J. Church. New York: Liberal Arts Press, 1951. https://archive.org /details/PlatosPhaedo1954/page/n25/mode/2up.

———. *The Republic of Plato.* Translated by A. D. Lindsay. London: J. M. Dent and Sons, 1923. https:// archive.org/details/therepublicofpla00platuoft/page/226/mode/2up.

———. *The Symposium.* Translated by M. C. Howatson. Cambridge, UK: Cambridge University Press, 2008. https://philarchive.org/archive/FREAR-4.

———. *The Theaetetus of Plato.* Translated by S. W. Dyde. Glasgow: James MacLehose and Sons, 1899. https:// www.google.com/books/edition/The_Theaetetus_of_Plato/wt29k-Jz8pIC?hl=en&gbpv=1&dq.

———. *The Timaeus of Plato.* Translated by R. D. Archer-Hind. London: MacMillan, 1888. https://archive .org/details/timaeusofplato00platiala/page/n5/mode/2up.

Porter, Stanley E., and Christopher D. Stanley, eds. *As It Is Written: Studying Paul's Use of Scripture.* Society of Biblical Literature Symposium Series 50. Atlanta: Society of Biblical Literature, 2008.

Porter, Stanley E., and Sean A. Adams, eds. *Paul and the Ancient Letter Form.* Leiden, NL: E. J. Brill, 2010.

Quinn, Jerome D. *The Letter to Titus.* Anchor Bible. Garden City, NY: Doubleday, 1990.

Robbins, Vernon K. *Exploring the Texture of Texts: A Guide to Socio-Rhetorical Interpretation*. Harrisburg, PA: Trinity Press International, 1996.

Schrenk, G. *patēr*. Pages 945-1022 in vol. 5 of *Theological Dictionary of the New Testament*. Edited by Gerhard Kittel and Gerhard Friedrich. Translated by Geoffrey W. Bromiley. Grand Rapids: Eerdmans, 1967.

Stott, John R. W. *The Message of 1 Timothy and Titus*. Downers Grove, IL: InterVarsity Press, 1996.

Stowers, S. K. *Letter Writing in Greco-Roman Antiquity*. Philadelphia: Westminster Press, 1986.

Thiselton, A. C. *The First Epistle to the Corinthians: A Commentary on the Greek Text*. Grand Rapids: Eerdmans, 2000.

Towner, Philip H. *1–2 Timothy and Titus*. The IVP New Testament Commentary Series. Downers Grove, IL: InterVarsity Press, 1994.

———. *The Letters to Timothy and Titus*. The New International Commentary on the New Testament. Grand Rapids: Eerdmans, 2006.

Truesdale, Al, ed. *Global Wesleyan Dictionary of Theology*. Kansas City: Beacon Hill Press of Kansas City, 2013.

Verner, David C. *The Household of God: The Social World of the Pastoral Epistles*. Society of Biblical Literature Dissertation Series 71. Chico, CA: Scholars Press, 1983.

Walker, Peter. "Revisiting the Pastoral Epistles—Part I." *European Journal of Theology* 21, no. 1 (2012): 4-16.

———. "Revisiting the Pastoral Epistles—Part II." *European Journal of Theology* 21, no. 2 (2012): 120-32.

Wallace, Daniel B. *Greek Grammar beyond the Basics*. Grand Rapids: Zondervan, 1996.

Wesley, John. "Predestination Calmly Considered." In vol. 10 of *The Works of John Wesley*, 3rd ed., edited by Thomas Jackson, 204-59. London: Wesleyan Methodist Book Room, 1872. Reprint, Peabody, MA: Hendrickson, 1984.

———. *The Works of John Wesley*. 3rd ed., edited by Thomas Jackson. 14 vols. London: Wesleyan Methodist Book Room, 1872. Reprint, Peabody, MA: Hendrickson, 1984.

Willis, Wendell L. *Idol Meat in Corinth: The Pauline Argument in 1 Corinthians 8 and 10*. Society of Biblical Literature Dissertation Series 68. Chico, CA: Scholars Press, 1985.

Winter, Bruce W. *Roman Wives, Roman Widows: The Appearance of New Women and the Pauline Communities*. Grand Rapids: Eerdmans, 2003.

Witherington, Ben, III. *Conflict and Community in Corinth: A Socio-Rhetorical Commentary on 1 and 2 Corinthians*. Grand Rapids: Eerdmans, 1995.

———. *1 and 2 Thessalonians: A Socio-Rhetorical Commentary*. Grand Rapids: Eerdmans, 2006.

———. *The Letters to Philemon, the Colossians, and the Ephesians: A Socio-Rhetorical Commentary on the Captivity Epistles*. Grand Rapids: Eerdmans, 2007.

———. *Women in the Earliest Churches*. Society for New Testament Studies Monograph Series 59. Cambridge, UK: Cambridge University Press, 1988.

Yonge, Charles Duke, with Philo of Alexandria. *The Works of Philo: Complete and Unabridged*. Peabody, MA: Hendrickson, 1995.